THE STRAIGHT PATH

THE STRAIGHT PATH

How to Survie Life's Confusions

MUBARAK SULAIMAN UKASHAT, PH.D.

Paperback Edition December 14, 2024
ISBN 979-8-9917919-9-1

DEDICATION

From the very depths of my heart, my consciousness, and my soul, I want to dedicate this work firstly to Almighty Allāh, the essence of my life, my first love, and the source of all the knowledge and energy that I have poured into this work, and secondly, to my parents whose unimaginable support has made it possible for me to get to this height in life. Lastly, to my lovely wife and children for changing my entire world.

Acknowledgments

"In the name of Allāh, The Most Beneficent, The Most Merciful"

THE beginning and completion of this book would have been nearly impossible without the invaluable support and guidance of close friends and family. My heartfelt thanks go to Eseoghene Al-Farūq Ohwojeheri, Jamal Sheeth Olalekan, Suleiman Mustapha Aleakwe, Abdul-Ali Abdulqadir Danesi, Muhammad Musa Mubarak, Farouk Ayodeji Al-Egbawiy, Abdul-Hafiz Sanni, Vaneesa Cook, Mahmud Tukur, Henry Dankwa, Rukaya Yakubu, Aisha Abdullahi, and Saʿadat Mohammed. I sincerely appreciate your help, cooperation, and understanding, which were essential to this endeavor. Your relentless support, encouragement, and the time many of you devoted to the success and completion of this book were invaluable. I am also grateful for your meticulous reviews, proofreading, annotations, and understanding.

I want to acknowledge the extraordinary debt I owe to my siblings, uncles, aunts, cousins, nephews, and nieces. Thank you all for your unwavering generosity in offering the best advice and moral and financial support anyone could hope for, for the beautiful moments we have shared, and for the effort you put into bringing out the best in me. Your contributions have been immense, and I recognize that my achievements would be incomplete without your brotherhood and spiritual guidance. You've all been wonderful, and I pray that Allāh blesses you and continues to guide you.

I am grateful to all the religious and academic institutions and communities I have participated in Nigeria. In Abuja, I thank Alhudā Islāmiyyah, Annūr Masjid, ICICE, One Ummah, Glisten International Academy, Abuja Preparatory School, AMIS, and Playhouse Daycare. I also extend my unreserved gratitude to FID in Lagos, the Islamic Centre in Ebonyi, PTI and FUPRE in Warri.

In Saudi Arabia, I want to thank King Fahd University of Petroleum and Minerals (KFUPM), the Islamic University in Madīnah, and the Masjid of 'Utbah Ibn Ghazwān in Dammam.

In the United States, I am grateful to Utah State University, Salt Lake Community College, Logan Islamic Centre, the Khadījah Masjid community, the Islamic Center of Kuwait, Annūr Masjid, and Madīnah Masjid, all in Utah.

I hope to repay you all one day for your unwavering love and support. Only Allāh knows where I would be without your help.

Mubarak Sulaiman Ukashat

Introduction

PEOPLE go through life on autopilot.

A simple question like, **'What do you want?'** can confuse more people than one would imagine. Often, the answer they provide is only relevant for the moment. Ask the same person again a few days later, and you may receive a completely different response, far from the initial one.

The truth is, people do not know what they want or where they are headed. This lack of clarity often stems from not having deeply considered these questions, mainly because they have not given these things the necessary thought or the needed time to mull them over.

Perhaps people need to be guided more than they need to be themselves. Perhaps people need to be shown the way rather than left to their lonesome, trying to map it out, especially when their lives are at stake. This is not about mind control, brainwashing, or indoctrination; it is about using the resources of the mind wisely instead of reinventing the wheel.

For thousands of years, humanity has sought answers about life.

Why should every generation start from scratch? What if there is already a path laid out? What if the knowledge of previous generations has been preserved, allowing others to build on their insights?

This collective knowledge is what we call history, heritage, and wisdom—an invaluable resource rather than a waste of experience.

Instead of relying on fallible men—from generation to generation—to chart this course for the good of posterity, imagine if God, the Knower of all, provided us with direction, offering us a map so we could focus on the journey itself. After all, even when we know the desired route we need to take, the journey is still not easy. In this book, the assertion is that this route is known as **The Straight Path**, which can help us navigate the complexities of life.

Muslims have the flexibility to pray at any time. Still, at specific times of the day, they are required to perform five daily prayers (As-salāt)[1]. Within these prayers, they can recite any part of the Qur'ān[2,3] they choose. However,

---

[1]a generic name for a ritual prayer of Muslims (made five times daily and can also refer to specific voluntary ones that are similar as well) in a standing position alternating with inclinations and prostrations as the worshiper faces toward Makkah.

[2]The Islamic sacred book, containing the word of God as revealed and dictated to Muhammad by the archangel Gabriel (Jibrīl) and written down in Arabic.

[3]We shall be using these long vowel sounds for proper Arabic word pronunciations. "ā" is the long "ahh" sound as in English "father", "ī" is like the "ee" in English "sheep" and "ū" is like the "oo" in "moon".

one mandatory chapter must be recited first; this chapter is called **Al-Fātiha**, or 'The Opening,' the first chapter of the Qur'ān.

The verses of Al-Fātiha begin by praising Allāh (God), expressing gratitude, and acknowledging His attributes. Following this, Muslims pledge their devotion and reliance on His help with all their affairs. This leads to the fundamental prayer:

"Guide us to the straight path."[4]

It is customary in Islamic tradition to praise and thank Allāh before requesting His blessings. This mirrors how people often interact; one might greet you, express gratitude for past assistance, acknowledge your kindness, and then make another momentary request. The salutations at the beginning of Alfātiha seem to prepare the ground for the main request:

"Guide us to the straight path."

Consider the significance of this sequence in our requests.

The Prophet Muhammad, God's peace and blessings be upon him (henceforth PBUH) reported in a Hadīth[5] Qudsī[6] that Allāh (God) said the following about this prayer,

---

[4] Every quotation from the Qur'ān in English used in this book is an interpretation of the meaning. The translation used, unless otherwise referenced, is "The Noble Qur'ān" by Muhammad Muhsin Khan and Muhammad Taqi-ud-Dīn al-Hilālī.

[5] Hadīth is a collection of traditions containing sayings of the Prophet Muhammad (PBUH) which, with accounts of his daily practices (Sunnah), constitute the major source of guidance for Muslims apart from the Qur'ān.

[6] Also known as the Sacred Narration, although separate from the Qur'ān, it is also attributed to Allāh, The Most High, and related from

"I have divided prayer between Myself and My servant into two halves, and My servant shall have what he has asked for. When the servant says, 'All praise is due to Allāh the Lord of the worlds,' Allāh says: My servant has praised Me. When he says, 'The Gracious, the Merciful,' Allāh says: My servant has exalted Me. When he says, 'The Master of the Day of Judgment,' Allāh says: My servant has glorified Me, and My servant has submitted to Me. When he says, 'You alone we worship, You alone we ask for help,' Allāh says: This is between Me and My servant, and My servant will have what he has asked for. When he says, 'Guide us to the straight path, the path of those whom you have favored, not those who earned Your wrath and those who went astray,' Allāh says: This is for My servant, and My servant will have what he has asked for."[7]

Him. The Messenger of Allāh (PBUH) would receive the meaning from Allāh, by way of inspiration or dream, and then he (PBUH) would inform his community of this in his own words.

[7] Ṣaḥīḥ Muslim, Hadīth No. 395

CONTENTS

01

Confusion; the Certainty about Nothing

Most declarations and motivational quotes often fail to endure over time. Frequently, flaws are revealed in the very lines of reasoning we once believed held the solutions to our problems. Sometimes, even the originators of these quotes come to realize that life is far more complex and confusing than they initially thought.

Perhaps, the hallmark of the modern era is the prevalence of confusion. Many people are uncertain about their feelings, doubt their sincerity, and question their own identities. Some do not even know what they truly believe and, as such, identify as indecisive, then settle in as *agnostics*.

The average person lacks a deep understanding of themselves, rendering the phrase *"man, know thyself"* a profound statement rather than a given. Even for the small demographic who claim to know themselves and can proclaim the certainty of their purpose, we can almost all agree that people are not what they truly say they are. While some may be outright liars, the more significant underlying issue is the enduring confusion that stems from a lack of clarity about self, life, and personal purpose.

In diagnosing confusion, doctors assert that one of the first signs is delirium, characterized by difficulty paying attention or focusing. Recent scientific studies indicate that the average attention span is declining[1]. From this, we can infer that confusion arises from our diminishing ability to focus.

The genuine gripe here is that we often do not know what to prioritize or focus on because we are overloaded with information and simulations. If people could clearly identify what matters most in life—without dispute— everyone could concentrate on that singular thing, eliminating confusion from their lives.

Unfortunately, these days, everything seems debatable. Confusion is evident not only among those who are yet to find themselves but also among those who have, as they grapple with questions of certainty and personal conviction, striving to ensure they are not deluding themselves. They hesitate between remaining the same, unchanged, or adapting to seemingly better options, unsure of the benchmarks to use for evaluating and appraising what is truly good. This intellectual confusion fosters a culture of ques-

---

[1]Gloria Mark, Attention Span: A Groundbreaking Way to Restore Balance, Happiness, and Productivity (2023)

tioning everything, leading some to identify as inherently *confused* or *agnostic*.

We can take one of three paths:

- **Certainty without doubt:** Some people are so convinced of their own understanding that they become what Nigerians, in their slang, informally refer to as ITK (short for I Too Know), failing to recognize the limits of their knowledge and adopting a rigid mindset.

- **Perpetual questioning:** Others approach everything with an overly indecisive and wavering mindset, never taking a definitive stand and believing that anyone could be right or wrong at any given moment, depending on various factors. Both extremes can lead to even greater confusion and difficulty in truly understanding life's events.

- **The balanced middle course:** This path involves being confident about specific core beliefs while remaining flexible about others. Being certain about specific things is defined as having a Foundational Creed. This Foundational Creed represents the essential tenets of one's faith, held even amidst uncertainty.

This *"Middle Course"* aligns with the concept of *"The Straight Path"*

The Foundational Creed–Certainty about Certain Things

A Foundational Creed consists of certain beliefs that may not be fully provable but are espoused and held with reasonable confidence. In everyday life, we accept many reductionist versions of such beliefs without question, even if we do not have all the requisite information to defend or prove their veracity. But once the topic is on religion, people become biased and may call it foolishness. For example, it is not considered foolish to assume that your mother loves you because, at its very crux, it is normal, reoccurring, and logical enough to make that easy assumption with a measure of faith despite the existence of some mothers who do not. This assumption is widely accepted and grounded in a common understanding of maternal affection.

Similarly, when you consult a doctor who prescribes medication to be dispensed by a pharmacist, it is not seen as irrational to trust that the medication is good and benefits you. You are neither expected to investigate the doctor's educational background and the manufacturing processes of the prescription nor scrutinize the pharmacist's motives, especially after reviewing both of their family's history and possible biases, to see if the medication is safe for ingestion. Such skepticism would likely be deemed excessive and even lead to questions about your mental state. As a matter of fact, if you do this, some might call the authorities to have you confined to a mental facility. Instead, we trust the qualifications of medical professionals simply because they work in established, reputable institutions.

Yet, when it comes to belief in God—despite the evident signs of His existence in nature and sacred texts—some deem it unwise to believe without having seen Him. Even if one did see Him and He made things manifest before their eyes, questions would arise about the reality of that experience. *Was the gazing upon His Glorious Visage simulated or real?* If they say it is real, others might proceed to ask what truly is real.

These all point to the need for us to establish certain belief systems or truths that are not 100 percent humanly provable. After all, even what we consider "proof" can be a source of disagreement and prone to dispute, leaving those who seek evidence for everything trapped in a cycle of confusion and uncertainty. Their lives are suffused with questions—of varying degrees and intensities—that might lead to other questions, resulting in a life of countless puzzles, so much so that they live life and leave it in a confused state, unfulfilled.

Having a Foundational Creed allows for accepting certain truths and beliefs upheld as undeniable truths that may not be entirely proven through our limited human abilities, intellectual resources, and experiences. This is vital for achieving clarity in life. When this creed represents the ultimate truth, it places everything else in perspective, helping to alleviate the confusion that often pervades our existence.

The Arguments for the Existence of a Creator, or 'God'.

The core tenets of Atheism emphasize the free use of common sense. However, this seems limited to mere utterance, as common sense comes up short when asked simple questions, like how the observable Universe came about without a Creator, for example. Such queries pose a huge challenge to Atheists.

When someone says, rather flippantly, *"You cannot prove the existence of God."*, Most people might mean theists cannot furnish a convincing philosophical argument for the existence of God. Agreed, but this does not tell us anything about God; instead, it only informs more about the *'nature of proof'* than it does about the existence of God. The inability to provide a persuasive argument, enough to convince everyone, without a shred of misgiving, that God exists is certainly not the problem. You see, it is—in a similar fashion—impossible to bring forth a fool-proof argument for any interesting philosophical conclusion such that everyone will accept it without a tinge of doubt.

We cannot certainly prove beyond the possibility of doubt—in a way that will convince all philosophers—that the mountains and rivers we see around us are really here, existing as mind-independent objects. We cannot prove that the entire universe did not come into existence five minutes ago and that all of our apparent memories are not illusions. We cannot prove that the other people we see in our neighborhood have minds. Perhaps they are very clever humanoids, high-performance robots. We cannot even prove that we are not some advanced version of *'Tom and Jerry'* with our producer and maker watching us on His higher-dimensional screen as he switches from one episode to another and periodically updates our software program every time we fall asleep, unconscious.

There are but a few interesting philosophical conclusions that can be proven beyond the possibility of doubt. Therefore, the fact that arguments for the existence of God do not conduce to mathematical certainty does not by itself weaken the case for the potency of God's existence. It simply poses the question of God's existence in the same category as these other philosophical questions, such as the existence of the external, mind-independent world and the tugging question of how we know other people possess minds. It becomes even more understandable when we realize how many of these different philosophical arguments we have come to terms with, accepting certain comfortable answers without seeking any further proof.

Consequentially, the inability to provide a compelling argument, one that convinces all thinking people, should never imply—even remotely—that we do not have tangible reason to believe in the existence of God. It might turn out, after your perusal, that some of the reasons for believing in God might be cogent enough for you. Even if you are not persuaded to believe in the existence of God, it still does not make the argument pointless.

It is reasonable to think that the mountains are real, our memories are generally reliable, and that other minds exist. It is logical to believe these assertions even if they are unprovable and not distillable through a scientific mesh. Maybe some argument for God's existence might persuade you that believing in God is reasonable.

Contrary to what some scientists claim, there is compelling philosophical, scientific, and evidential credence that a Creator of the Universe exists.

1. Argument from the Existence of Scientific Laws

Many scientists conduct their research without ever considering profound philosophical questions such as: 'Why do we have laws, instead of complete chaos?' or 'Why are the laws of nature the same throughout the entire universe?' Most scientists, by default, assume that laws exist and that they are worth discovering. This presumption forms the foundation of their work.

Take, for example, the scientific description of the atom. We are told that atoms are composed of particles like protons and neutrons and that these particles are themselves made up of even smaller units called quarks. This scientific explanation accounts for the structure and the physical-chemical behavior of atoms. However, it does not address the deeper question: *'Why do these laws govern reality, instead of chaos?'*

Indeed, the existence of natural laws is undeniable. But the question remains: What explains these laws? This is where two broad worldviews come into play: theism and materialist atheism. Theism provides a more coherent explanation for the existence of these laws. A rational, conscious, omnipotent lawmaker offers a far more convincing reason for the existence of laws in nature than does the materialist-atheist perspective. Furthermore, the idea of a single, omnipotent lawmaker helps explain why these laws are consistent across the entire universe.

2. Argument from the Laws of Thermodynamics

All unidirectional processes signal an inevitable end. The aging of humans and the increase of entropy in the universe are both irreversible. The entropy of the universe continues to rise, steadily and without reversal. As a result, the universe will ultimately reach thermodynamic equilibrium, often referred to as the 'heat death.'

In other words, the universe is not eternal; it has a

finite lifespan. If the past were truly infinite, thermodynamic equilibrium would already have been achieved, and all motion would have ceased. Yet we observe that motion is still occurring. Therefore, the universe cannot be eternal—it must have had a beginning.

Scientists often focus on the implications of entropy for the eventual end of the universe but they tend to overlook its implications for the universe's beginning

For example, the conditions prescribed by the first and second laws of thermodynamics demand special creation. The Second Law states that the universe must have had a monitored beginning—otherwise, it would have been completely disordered. The First Law (conservation of mass-energy) says it could not have begun by its own volition or making.

On this point, Paul Davies says:

"It is clear that if the universe is irreversibly running down at a finite rate, then it cannot have existed forever. The reason is simple: if the universe were infinitely old, it would have died already. Something that runs down at a finite rate obviously cannot have existed for eternity. In other words, the universe must have come into existence a finite time ago. It is remarkable that this profound conclusion was not properly grasped by the scientists of the nineteenth century."[2]

3. The Fine-Tuning Argument

One version of the fine-tuning argument postulates that the natural laws governing the material world encom-

---

[2] Paul Davies, The Last Three Minutes, Basic Books, New York, 1994.

pass fundamental constants. These numbers are precisely calibrated for the existence of intelligent life, and if any of them deviated by even by a wee fraction, stars, planets, chemistry, and living things could never have existed. The One, by Whose Might the universe was formed, cannot be subject to these numbers—of Time and Space —since He fashioned and stipulated their limits in the first place.

4. The Discoverability and Potentiality of the Universe Argument

The discoverability of the universe argument asserts that human beings, despite their limitations, are able to make significant discoveries about the universe. Theism provides a better explanation because it accounts for the mathematical structure of the universe, the presence of laws that enable discoverability, the development of tools for exploration, and the existence of evidence that guides scientific inquiry. The argument uses examples like radiocarbon dating and other scientific clues, suggesting that these signs exist for a reason. Theism posits that a conscious design is behind the universe's discoverability, making it a more coherent explanation than materialist atheism.

The potentiality of the universe argument highlights that the universe's potentiality—its capacity to give rise to diverse things—is fundamental to everything that exists. Just as Lego blocks have limited potential to form certain structures, the universe has the potential to form stars, plants, animals, human creations, and more. The question is why the universe possesses such vast potential. Theism offers a better explanation because it aligns with the idea that a conscious creator designed the universe with the potential for beauty, rationality, and consciousness. Theism also explains the existence of beauty and human reason in the universe, as these are expected in a universe created by God. In contrast, materialist atheism struggles to account for these aspects, making the theistic view more plausible.

In conclusion, the argument asserts that the diverse and meaningful aspects of the universe, from art to reason, are made possible by its potentiality, which is best explained by theism as the product of a conscious creator, rather than by random chance or materialist-atheism.

5. The Trivial Logical Argument (Pascal's Wager)

Developed by Blaise Pascal, a 17th-century French mathematician, physicist, theologian, and philosopher, Pascal's Wager is a philosophical argument that suggests it is more rational and prudent to believe in God. This argument draws upon concepts from the probability theory, decision theory, pragmatism, and voluntarism. According to Pascal, a believer in God stands to gain if God exists, losing nothing if He does not. In contrast, a disbeliever in the existence of God loses nothing if God does not exist, but risks losing everything if He does. From this perspective, it appears more logical, more cogent, to wager on the existence of God. However, this argument reduces belief to a gamble. Faith in God is far more profound, and as Muslims, we seek more substantial reasons to believe in Allāh.

6. The Ultimate Justice Argument

Another argument for God's existence lies in the concept of ultimate justice, which ensures fairness in judgment for criminals who escape earthly justice. This argument posits it is logical and morally sound to believe in an afterlife where ultimate justice is served, wherein their victims in this life might have their rights and dignity restored while the oppressors are penalized accordingly. The limitations and defects in the human justice system further reinforce this idea. It cannot provide commensurate rewards or punishments for good or evil, respectively.

For example, say, a criminal was responsible for the death of millions. Even if they were captured and subsequently sentenced to death, that one death would never possibly atone for the millions of lives lost. This here is where the Quranic verses come into play, describing how the scarred fleshes of the dwellers of Hell are burned through, only to be replenished to repeat their suffering anew. Under such justice, they would suffer the commensurate requisite consequences for every life they destroyed, every victim accounted for.

7. The Existence of Source or Ontological Argument

Another powerful proof of God's existence lies in the word **'existence'** itself. Just as it is often said that *"like begets like,"* theists argue that life cannot come from anything other than something living. If humans exist as living beings, then so must a Higher power Who serves as the source of life, understands life, and makes it possible for us and all other living beings to also exist and experience life or *'existence'*.

The main ideas supporting this view include:

- **Complexity of life:** Some consider the intricate mechanisms of life—from the ornate structure of DNA to the human brain—too finely tuned to have been a product created solely by chance, suggesting—deductively—a guiding intelligence.

- **Self-awareness:** Some consider the human ability to think, reason, and experience subjective experiences like emotions a unique attribute that points towards a spiritual dimension far beyond the palpable physical world.

- **Moral sense:** The innate human sense of right and wrong, or morality, is often used as evidence for a higher moral standard established by a divine being.

8. The Revelation Argument

First, like in all the previous arguments, we can infer what might be true about God from what we observe in the universe. We look at the physical universe, human nature, and culture and observe things that may be clues to the existence or nature of the supernatural.

Another angle to finding God is inherent in the fact that He may have revealed Himself to us through His prophets and messengers and told us true things about Himself, His morality, His meaning, and how to have a relationship with Him. This is called Revelation.

This is one of the most significantly logical reasons Muslims can propound as proof of God's existence, especially for those who remain unmoved by the plethora of telling signs around us.

Atheists often claim that if God exists, they will tell Him—straightforwardly—upon their resurrection that He did not provide sufficient evidence of His existence. This argument is fundamentally incoherent, especially in the light of what is to follow.

One might argue there is no physical evidence for the existence of God, but how about the physical evidence for the existence of His Prophet, Muhammad (PBUH)? If you acknowledge that Muhammad (PBUH) existed, then you cannot reasonably repudiate the existence of God, as Muhammad (PBUH) had proclaimed he received revelations from God through His Angel. The right question to now follow is,

"Have you taken your time to truly consider this message?"

Not believing in God is weird and painfully misinformed. For anything, it is closing the mind solely on the premise of *"I am yet to see convincing evidence."* For the Believer, tell-tale signs are evidence enough to prove there is more to the observable Universe than meets the eye; there's more to stir their educated resolve.

The worst an Atheist could say—admissibly—is that 'Something' caused, inspired, the entire creation process to happen, even as the said 'Thing' remains unknown. Indeed, some Atheists have come to accept this, ringing off about *"an uncaused cause."* This inevitably makes every atheist agnostic, at best—someone who says he does not know. And the confusion continues.

This means the difference between atheists and theists is a case of saying, *"I do not know,"* and *"I think and believe so."* This counters some atheists' untenable argument that religious people are a doltish, highly impressionable, and susceptible lot. No, religious people have only not taken ignorance as their intellectual stance. Rather, they have accepted certain belief systems to guide them and have dared to make sense of life.[3]

Divine Guidance Through a Foundational Creed

Having addressed the major bone of contention as it relates to the foundational creed, the next question one might pose is:

What does this do for me?

How does believing in this make my life any better?

This is the main focus of this entire book, and we shall unravel the answers to these questions as we muster on. For starters, with a Foundational Creed, we can address the world's most confusing questions:

- *Why do people die?*

  Creed: They only shift basis, transition to another realm, embarking on a new journey.

- *Why do the wicked escape justice?*

  Creed: There will be a Day of Judgment when all will receive their due rewards and punishments, signaling a final closure.

---

[3]Some of the ideas expressed in this section were taken from https://www.icr.org/article/evidence-for-creator, https://gradresources.org/evidence-for-gods-existence/, and 12 Arguments for the Existence of God by Caner Taslaman

- *Why do good people suffer?*

  Creed: Their enduring struggles will be rewarded in the afterlife, leading them to wish they had endured even more in life's tribulations.

These are only examples, and for some, there is certainly more than one answer, but they illustrate how a Foundational Creed can provide clarity, offering straightforward answers that help navigate life's complexities.

In Arabic, this Foundational Creed is known as *Al-Aqīdah*. It is an amalgam of basic truths that represent the core beliefs you choose to uphold with certainty, illuminating your approach to various life aspects and keeping you focused in life on the most important things.

Before exploring Al-Aqīdah further, one might wonder if there can be more than one correct Creed. The answer is No since only one Creed boldly claims it can clarify all matters of existence. This Creed addresses the fundamental questions of life, providing guidance even when direct answers are not available. Its divine nature is supported by abundant evidence, especially its source and practical effectiveness, which we will discuss in later chapters.

In essence, the summary of what we must believe to follow the Straight Path is encapsulated in a verse of the Qur'ān when Allāh (God) says:

"The Messenger believes in what has been sent down to him from his Lord, and (so do) the believers. Each one believes in Allāh, His Angels, His Books and His Messengers. They say, 'We make no distinction between one and another of His Messengers'—and they say, 'We hear, and we obey. (We seek)

Your forgiveness, our Lord, and to You is the return (of all)." -
Qur'ān, 2:285

From the verse and various prophetic narrations, six key principles can be deduced to help guide our journey in this world along the desired path:

1. Belief in the Oneness of Allāh

2. Belief in His Angels

3. Belief in His Books

4. Belief in His Messengers

5. Belief in the Day of Judgment

6. Belief in the Divine Decree

Clarifying Life with Tawhīd (Oneness of Allāh)

Belief in Allāh's oneness involves recognizing Him as your Lord and accepting Him as the only one worthy of your worship and absolute obedience. You should also acknowledge His unique names and attributes. These divine qualities should guide every aspect of your life, sustaining you on the straight path.

Submitting to Allāh means placing the highest premium on His guidance, prioritizing it over your own desires, as you understand that He is your Creator and the One most deserving of shaping the direction of your life. You worship Him exclusively, placing nothing—not even yourself—above Him and refraining from associating any other deities in your worship (hence confusing yourself).

This commitment becomes the foundation for your existence, providing clear direction. If your life is centered on a single tenet, why not make it the service of your Creator? This is, indeed, the *Straight Path*.

To worship Him effectively, you must seek to know Him, which includes understanding His names and attributes. For instance, knowing Him as *Al-Wahhāb* (The Bestower) reminds you that he is the author of this straight path that He has enjoined on you. It further reassures you that following His straight path will lead to the best outcomes. You will quickly realize the inherent benefits of adhering to His commands and avoiding what He prohibits.

Recognizing Him as *Ar-Rahīm* (The Especially Merciful) and *Al-'Afuww* (The Pardoner) helps you not to be overwhelmed by your innumerable sins and faux pas. You can hold onto hope in His vast mercy, knowing that sincerity can earn you another chance. Understanding Him as Al-Hasīb (The Reckoner) reminds you that while He is forgiving, He is also the Most Just: One who will avenge everyone you oppress, ensuring that everyone you have wronged receives their due recompense.

When you encounter His attributes, as mentioned in the verse below, it deepens your understanding of Him, encouraging personal growth through your relationship with Him.

"Say, O Prophet, "O Allāh! Lord over all authorities! You give authority to whoever You please and remove it from who You please; You honor whoever You please, and disgrace who You please—all good is in Your Hands. Surely You alone are Most

Capable of everything." – Qur'ān, 3:26

You understand that only Allāh can humble you from any height He has granted you, instilling a sense of trepidation and humility within you. We will explore this further in a later chapter. The key takeaway is that once you accept Allāh as your Lord, recognizing that He alone deserves your worship and that nothing should come before Him, and once you know and understand His names and attributes, life will become crystal clear and will—like clockwork—click into place for you. Anything other than this, without this clarity, you may find yourself in a constant state of confusion about your direction and goals, driven and enslaved by your own shifting emotions and overwhelmed by the flood of information and realizations.

Certainty of Accountability

Some people believe reincarnation is the only fair way to address good or evil deeds and make sense of the unsettling realization, suggesting that those who commit terrible acts will return to this world and suffer in a different future life. However, consider the simplicity of believing in a final reckoning at the end of one's life. For example, if someone lives a life of untold evil without facing immediate retribution, why not hold them accountable after they die? Instead of a scenario in which they are reincarnated as a low-lifer with a miserable existence, as often claimed, a person could be required to give a full account of their actions and face proportionate punishment for their wrongdoings.

Is the latter not simpler and more logically coherent?

The belief in angels serves an important purpose. It instills in us a sense of accountability. These celestial beings constantly watch over humanity, recording our actions and serving as unseen witnesses to everything we do.

"Not a word does he (or she) utter, but there is a watcher by him ready (to record it)." - Qur'ān, 50:18

Allāh is fully aware of our actions, including those we have forgotten and the intentions we hold in our hearts.

"...Verily! Allāh is Witness over all things." - Qur'ān, 22:17

The presence of angels as witnesses fixates on the importance of justice. On the Day of Accountability, even our own body parts will testify.

"On the Day when their tongues, their hands, and their legs or feet will bear witness against them as to what they used to do. On that Day Allāh will pay them the recompense of their deeds in full, and they will know that Allāh, He is the Manifest Truth." - Qur'ān, 24:24-25

As the verse above shows, even though Allāh is All-Knowing and our own body parts will testify to our actions, He still sends angels to watch over us. One might wonder, *"Why is that?" But who can question His wisdom?* He provides multiple layers of evidence for His final judgment, like the layers of an onion. The point here is to establish justice, especially when no other authority exists above His to checkmate His Sovereignty.

Given this, should we not also be fair in our judgments of others, especially when our evidence is limited? Despite having all this proof, Allāh still forgives us. Believing in this should inspire us to forgive others too. There are many benefits in everything Allāh commands us to believe.

This idea also applies to the Day of Judgment. Knowing that every single action, even the smallest details, will be reviewed makes us more careful in our actions. Allāh could have simply judged everyone based on their final moments, but instead, He created a Day of Accountability. This shows His perfect justice and encourages us to give others a fair chance in life, appreciating Allāh's endless mercy.

Codified Guidance to Avoid Confusion

A key part of our foundational beliefs is trusting in the books revealed to guide humanity. For example, the Qur'ān serves as a divine guide. It does not say everything but offers a bird's-eye view of everything, providing a broad perspective and direction for our lives. It should be our reference for daily living.

The question then is: *why do we choose a particular book for guidance?* The simple and obvious answer is that we need guidance, and we must elect to relinquish our personal sovereignty to a Supreme Being for the needed guidance, which is communicated through an inimitable Book from Him. *How do we know the Qur'ān is from God?* The answer is simply because it proves itself by lending credence to that claim from within its verses. This claim might be quickly followed by disproval, saying that a thing cannot stand judge and jury on its own case except by the support of external proof or evidence outside of itself. But this assumption is wrong.

By way of analogy, imagine if your father penned a letter to you in which he addressed you by a strange name repeatedly. You certainly might doubt its credibility. This misgiving is created by a specific mistake in the letter's content. In the same way, if in the same letter, he mentioned something known only to both of you, it might provide tangible proof, enough to convince you that he was indeed the true sender. By such inference, a piece of writing can be self-evidential, like the Qur'ān is for itself.

"But Allāh bears witness to that which He has sent down (the Qur'ān) unto you (O Muhammad), He has sent it down with His Knowledge, and the angels bear witness. And Allāh is All-Sufficient as a Witness." – Qur'ān, 4:166

At first glance, one might think that claiming to be authentic is not proof enough. However, many books claiming to be from God do not even assert divine authenticity; they simply reflect human thoughts. Often, these books do not mention their titles anywhere within their verses. In contrast, the Qur'ān identifies itself by name about 70 times, unlike other books named centuries after their supposed revelation from the sanction of human authorities like Scribes and Kings or religious demagogues.

This section is not focused on proving the Qur'ān's authenticity, which will be discussed later. The key point here is the importance of having a reliable reference to guide our daily lives. Belief in divine books prevents anyone from waking up any given morning with wild claims of clairvoyance, saying that a spirit spoke to them and that the supposed voice is of God, giving justification to every one of their proclamations as proceeding from God, based solely on a dream. There would be, and are, many false prophets since such claims could give legitimacy to all kinds of wild assertions if they are accepted without question.

In Islām, there is a consistent foundation and a common provable denominator to be referenced in the search for truth: a single book that has remained unchanged over time and forms the basis of our beliefs. Since we believe that divine revelations have concluded with the last Prophet Muhammad (PBUH), we avoid unnecessary debates about claims of new revelations from God.

A Familiar Example

God has sent Prophets and messengers from among people— ordinary, fallible humans who are not to be worshiped. Their role is to share God's message and model the best moral behavior. This makes sense because humans are social beings and tend to emulate others like themselves.

If God had sent angels, who are consistently obedient and compliant because they lack free will, people might feel that their example is unattainable: "They are angels, after all." The lives of these messengers provide a clear guide for us. Instead of over-analyzing our lives for truth and falsehood, we can follow the proven example of these messengers, doing what they did and avoiding what they avoided. There is no need to reinvent the wheel.

"Indeed in the Messenger of Allāh (Muhammad) you have a good example to follow for him who hopes in (the Meeting with) Allāh and the Last Day and remembers Allāh much." - Qur'ān, 33:21

From them, we learn what good character looks like for us to follow and emulate.

"And verily, you (O Muhammad) are on an exalted standard of character." - Qur'ān, 68:4

Some might think identifying good character is easy, but living among people makes it more complex. For instance, being friendly and visiting others freely might seem admirable, even walking through their doors unannounced, so close to them that you do not need their say-so to enter their space. How be it, then, that the Prophet Muhammad (PBUH) advised that if you visit someone and knock three times without a response, you should leave without holding a grudge.[4] This respects their need for privacy or time alone, and acting overly friendly may sometimes burden others.

Even those who spent much quality time with the Prophet, despite being in the best company anyone would wish for, their long visits sometimes became a burden for him. To handle this gently, Allāh revealed:

"O you who believe! Enter not the Prophet's houses, except when leave is given to you for a meal, (and then) not (so early as) to wait for its preparation. But when you are invited, enter, and when you have taken your meal, disperse without sitting for a talk. Verily, such (behavior) annoys the Prophet, and he is shy about (asking) you (to go), but Allāh is not shy about (telling you) the truth. ...." – Qur'ān, 33:53

---

[4]Ṣaḥīḥ al-Bukhārī, Hadīth No. 6245

In this verse, we see the Prophet's humility, a quality we should emulate. He gracefully endured discomfort and felt too shy to ask people to leave, even though they revered him and would likely have understood. This teaches us that while spending time with good company is great, we should also respect their personal time and know when to step back.

This example is just one of many from which we can learn about the straight path in life, teaching us new ways of appraising our moral values and being considerate of others. This is from the wisdom of sending Messengers. Their stories guide us, showing us how to strive to be the best versions of ourselves, knowing that if they can do it, so can we.

A Balanced Pursuit with Faith in Destiny

How should we make sense of our goals in life? How should we view our desires, especially for what we covet? We often work hard but do not always get what we want. How do we know our limits?

The answers lie in the belief in predestination: everything is meant to unfold in a certain way. We trust that what is meant for us, whether good or bad, will reach us, and we will not miss out on what is meant for us (and the opposite is true). This belief keeps us from becoming desperate in our pursuits, reminding us that outcomes are not solely in our control. This way, we are not desperate to go beyond the protective confines of our faith to achieve our life goals.

"Man proposes, God disposes" is a useful saying to remind us of the futility of wanting our way.

For instance, we might deeply desire a child and do everything possible, including seeking medical help, yet still not conceive. We may even stand mighty in prayers, all day and all night, and still never conceive. For those who struggle with the idea of divine predestination, this can be crushing. But those who accept it and have faith in God's ultimate will can find peace, knowing that God, in His perfect knowledge, may have other plans and hence decreed otherwise.

"To Allāh belongs the kingdom of the heavens and the earth. He creates what He wills. He bestows female (offspring) upon whom He wills, and bestows male (offspring) upon whom He wills. Or He bestows both males and females, and He renders barren whom He wills. Verily, He is the All-Knower and is Able to do all things." - Qur'ān, 42:49-50

What about our efforts in striving and relentless praying?
Islām provides clarity: we are rewarded for every moment spent in prayer, for trusting Allāh's divine plan, and for being patient during tough times, even in our loss of fortune. The key point is to remain calm and confident even when our hopes are repeatedly dashed, accepting with conviction that perhaps Allāh has decreed it that way.

This also applies to our hard work in earning a living. If you have put in your best effort, improving and trying your hardest, yet find yourself struggling more than others who seem to work less, remember Allāh's words:

"Allāh enlarges the provision for whom He wills of His slaves, and straitens it for whom (He wills). Verily, Allāh is the All-Knower of everything." - Qur'ān, 29:62

We learn that Allāh gives to those who He wills, based on His infinite wisdom, not just to those who work hardest.

So why do we work hard?

To fulfill our part, we must ensure we are not to blame if things do not go as planned. Our sincere efforts may lead to rewards we cannot always see.

A Muslim who believes this will not be confused when life does not sail their boat in the direction of their choosing. Even when life does not seem to reward their hard work, they persist in trying and praying, accepting whatever outcome might be—good or bad—while trusting that things will ultimately turn out for the best.

In contrast, some other faiths equate material success with God's love, a crude appraisal that oversimplifies His vast mercy. Islām teaches that Allāh alone knows why He chooses to give some people, regardless of their faith. This explains why even atheists who do not believe in God can still have abundance. Worldly wealth cannot measure one's worth since our true worth is only known to God and will only be revealed in the afterlife.

It is important to remember that this worldly life is insignificant compared to the afterlife. As the Prophet (PBUH) said,

"Were this world worth a wing of a mosquito in the sight of Allāh, He would not have given the disbeliever a drink of water thereof."[5]

Imagine an aggressor coming into your home, insulting you, and trying to steal your belongings. You would

---

[5] Sunan al-Tirmidhī, Hadīth No. 2320

not reward their bad behavior and might attempt to stop them from doing that, especially when you are evidently stronger. If they end up stealing something worthless, say your trash, for instance, you might not care. The entire wealth of this world is likened to that worthless trash when compared to the reward of the afterlife. Allāh may not punish you by depriving you of worldly wealth because it is trivial in comparison to what you stand to lose in the hereafter from disbelief.

Sometimes, Allāh grants wealth as a blessing for both this life and the next. We may not always know if the wealth we possess is a blessing or not, but we can find peace in submitting to Allāh's decisions and being grateful for what we have.

At this point, you might feel we are straying into abstract faith, but if you reflect a bit longer, you will see how these principles apply to daily life. There is no situation that cannot be resolved with these beliefs; it is a complete way of life that offers clarity in every aspect if we pay attention.

"So be patient (O Muhammad). Verily, the Promise of Allāh is true, and let not those who have no certainty of faith, discourage you from conveying Allāh's Message (which you are obliged to convey)." - Qur'ān, 30:60

02

PAYING ATTENTION, RECOGNIZING SIGNS ALONG THE WAY

IT is often said that the best place to hide something is in plain sight; if you want to keep something from being found, conceal it where it would normally be easy to see.

For example, if you do not want someone to find your car keys, you would not hide them under the bed—those are expected places to check. Instead, you might hang them on the door, their usual exit point, which they are unlikely to consider. The search for missing keys leads them to believe they must be hidden far away, causing them to overlook obvious locations.

This example narrows down to two points: first, we

often miss signs that are right in front of us while searching for clues elsewhere. Second, people tend to overlook what is directly in their line of sight, staring them right in the face. Our minds often seek out complexities before accepting simplicities.

This tendency to overlook the obvious explains why people frequently ask God for signs, even when they are all around us, going off like sirens and shining like carnival lights. Days and nights pass, and as we step outside, we gaze up at the vast expanse we often take for granted, this monstrous phenomenon and body of materials we flippantly dismiss as "the sky." This is even when we give ourselves a little ruminating time if we ever do. Many people can go an entire day without giving it a second thought, despite its constant influence on our lives—cloudy days, rain, and sunny skies come and go in a cycle, yet the average person remains largely indifferent to them.

"Verily, in the alternation of the night and the day and in all that Allāh has created in the heavens and the earth are Āyāt (proofs, evidences, verses, lessons, signs, revelations, etc.) for those people who keep their duty to Allāh, and fear Him much." – Qur'ān, 10:6

It might be understandable if a fixed, immovable statue, however imposing and magnificent, fails to capture our interest. But, with its cyclical shifts between night and day and the breathtaking changes of the seasons, the sky continues to be overlooked by many. People often seek other signs of God's existence or evidence that a higher power governs the intricacies of our world. We do not see things even when they are too obvious—staring us right between the eyes—sometimes. This tendency is a reminder of why we must pay closer attention; otherwise, we risk missing profound signs and veering into confusion.

Consider someone trying to force-feed a hungry infant who refuses to eat. If you observe closely, you might understand the reasons behind the baby's reluctance, even amidst hunger. Sadly, most people tend to focus on the problem rather than its root cause. A mother who watches her baby over several months may quickly discern that the infant is uncomfortable due to a soiled diaper or simply needs to be held differently. Addressing these underlying issues, she can guide her baby back to happily eating.

As a Nigerian living in the U.S. and married to a woman of a different race, my wife unexpectedly pointed out my tendency to raise my voice during conversations. Initially, I was puzzled, thinking my tone was perfectly normal. However, some of my students and non-African friends also echoed her concern.

coincidentally, When my wife visited Nigeria for the first time, she immediately noticed that everyone's voice sounded up an octave; everyone seemed to speak at a higher volume than she was used to. Then, I realized that the equivalent of a Nigerian whisper could well mirror her family's conversational tone.

It became clear to me that I needed to adapt and embrace a more suitable cultural approach. As a Muslim, I began to wonder which of these two communication styles aligned more closely with the values of my faith.

Then, I remembered a verse from the Qur'ān where the honorable Luqmān was exhorting his son, and he said;

"And be moderate (or show no insolence) in your walking, and lower your voice. Verily, the harshest of all voices is the voice (braying) of the donkey." - Qur'ān, 31:19

From his advice, I realized it was wise to avoid being overly loud in my daily conversations. Had I not embraced Islām as my guiding creed (as my focus against confusion), I might still be grappling with this dilemma. Nationalism, racism, chauvinism, and my own ego were just a few of the 'isms' that could have clouded my judgment, especially without the clarity provided by the *"Straight Path."*

It is worth noting that I had recited and reflected on this same verse countless times, yet I never connected it to my own situation. This oversight was easy to make, as being loud is a daily experience among many in my home country, not allowing me to consider how it might come across as abrasive to others.

This reminds us to adhere to the straight path—a reliable framework that helps us avoid a confusing and aimless life. We should be willing to reassess our daily habits and cultural practices, even those we hold dear, in order to grow personally and in our consideration toward others. Just because something feels normal does not mean it is right or optimal; it is simply what we are accustomed to.

From my cultural background, a couple of aphorisms come to mind. The *Warri* people of South-Southern Nigeria often say in pidgin English, *"Okpolor eye, nor be open eye"* and *"Nor be who first call Police de win the case."* The first of these expressions conveys that bulging eyes do not necessarily mean better vision, just as being loud and boastful is not an indicator of true intellect. The latter implies that the one who initiates a case does not always emerge victorious.

These local maxims encourage us to look deeper into issues without the usual habit of following the obvious. After all, as the saying goes, *a book should not be judged by its cover.* There is wisdom in our culture, just as there are lessons to be learned from others, allowing us to refine our lives through learning, relearning, and unlearning.

We must not be swayed by first impressions. It is essential to critically assess matters, using our Creed as a guiding framework in defining the parameters to avoid confusion.

Yes, certain traits may feel innate and have been with you all your life, but are they truly beneficial?

Yes, your traditions shape your identity, but are they positive?

Yes, you might love certain aspects of your culture—they bring you joy—but are they the right things?

We need to adhere to the *'Straight Path'* by aligning our lives with the principles of our foundational Creed as Muslims, particularly as exemplified by the life of the Prophet Muhammad (PBUH). His wife, 'Āisha (may Allāh be pleased with her, R.A henceforth), noted that he embodied the teachings of the Qur'ān.[1] There are many ways to enhance our awareness, pay better attention, and improve our clarity along this Path:

---

[1]Musnad Imām Ahmad Page No. 25813

1. Mindfulness

At its core, mindfulness is about being fully present. Those from the past might struggle to grasp the challenges we face today in our fast-paced world, filled with distractions that make it difficult to stay fully focused in both body and soul. Unlike previous generations, with fewer options and distractions, people nowadays encounter constant stimuli vying for their attention.

For example, you might see someone in a park, earphones on, zoned in, deeply absorbed in conversations from far-flung corners of the world. In that moment, they are seldom not truly present. Whether these conversations are genuine or artificially created by technology, they draw focus away from the here and now.

Similarly, a person may be physically present but lost in a book about events happening elsewhere, allowing that narrative to overshadow the joy and laughter around them. The opposite can also be true. They might be surrounded by engaging conversation yet be mentally preoccupied with worries that have no direct connection to their current environment.

At its most relatable, mindfulness reminds us that people can be physically present but mentally absent, rattled by concerns that distract them from experiencing their immediate surroundings. It becomes even more concerning when we realize that individuals in these scenarios often do not recognize that their minds have wandered. Their responses are shaped by thoughts disconnected from their immediate surroundings, leading them to react differently from what is directly before them.

Mindfulness goes beyond simply being present; it involves being acutely aware of your thoughts and where your mind is at any given moment. This awareness can be profoundly transformative and powerful as a tool for behavior that is sometimes deployed to cure addiction. Instead of merely advising people to avoid unhealthy foods, for instance, we might encourage them to recall how terrible they feel after overeating those very foods.

We often feel remorse over actions that cause us distress, yet in the moment, we fail to focus on the deeper pains of the negative emotions and self-betrayal that follow. Too frequently, we distract ourselves or attribute our painful feelings to unrelated events.

If we take a moment to truly reflect on how we felt by acknowledging the significant emotional toll, the effect of our mistakes will hit us to the core in more ways, and we might be less inclined to repeat those behaviors. This can be seen when we make financial mistakes; although we resolve to be more cautious, we often revert to our old habits once things settle. However, if we remember the disappointment that accompanied those mistakes, we may be more committed to avoiding them in the future.

Consider the scenario where someone splurges on some inconsequentialities—the latest gizmos, for example—and then face a financial strain, unable to provide for their family. Here, the event, the feelings of regret, and the distress of failing in their primary responsibilities converge. The pain of seeing their family suffer from hunger can lead to a deep sense of hopelessness and regret, especially if they realize that better financial choices could have spared them this hardship.

In striving to avoid financial missteps in the future, it

may be more beneficial to focus on the pain of regret—*the emotional fallout*—rather than the *event itself.* This emphasizes the importance of understanding and being aware of your mind. When you find yourself absent-minded, it is crucial to recalibrate and recognize that you are not being mindful. This can help pull your focus back to the present, providing clarity to navigate your circumstances wisely.

To be mindful is to resist letting your mind drift toward distractions. It is a practice of thoughtful engagement and clear observation of your surroundings. A mindful individual acts only after careful consideration rather than impulsively.

When mixed, chemicals react without thought, often leading to chaotic results. Similarly, a fragile object left unattended will inevitably fall and shatter, as it lacks awareness of its own vulnerability. Just as this object cannot self-reflect, we can also fall into mindless actions if we engage in routines without understanding their significance or impact.

Being mindful means assessing situations thoughtfully and acting based on various considerations, ensuring you have observed, reflected, and prioritized the best options.

2. Observation

It has become increasingly common for people to overlook significant details, failing to truly recognize what they have seen or heard throughout their lives. This is particularly disheartening, as the information we absorb shapes our minds and, by extension, who we become. Imagine being influenced by things you do not fully understand—*how much control do you really have over your tendencies and the person you might ultimately become?*

Even within religious communities, it is not uncommon to find individuals who profess deep affection for their faith yet lack a fundamental understanding of its teachings. The phrase **"O you who believe…"**, as an example, appears over 80 times in the Qur'ān, specifically addressing Muslims. If you were to ask a Muslim from any community around the world to recall just five of these instances, you would likely be met with silence. This highlights a troubling degree of absent-mindedness, even concerning matters that are close to their hearts and right in front of them. The Qur'ān emphasizes the importance of listening.

"Those who listen to the Word and follow the best thereof, those are (the ones) whom Allāh has guided and those are men of understanding" - Qur'ān, 39:18

It takes it a step further by specifically using the phrase *"pay attention"* in the context of listening.

"So, when the Qur'ān is recited, listen to it, and be silent (paying attention) that you may receive mercy." - Qur'ān, 7: 204

Today, it is all too common to find individuals who profess love for their religion yet know far less about its teachings than they do about current affairs, such as pop culture, music, or reality television. While engaging with one's chosen creed is essential, prioritizing entertainment over the foundational principles that guide your life is counterproductive.

Moreover, entertainment often requires minimal focus, yet it gradually undermines our attention to genuinely important matters. This serves as a clear indication that such distractions may not be beneficial. They can divert our attention from what truly matters.

We began by discussing mindfulness because it is crucial for grasping the fundamental truths of our existence. Many individuals face challenges without extracting meaningful lessons from them—often because they lack the mindfulness necessary to recognize these insights. Observing is vital, as it helps us avoid distractions that cloud our judgment and distort our perception of reality. This points us the rationale behind Islām's prohibition of intoxicants, or mind-warpers, since they distort our sense of reality.

The prohibition on intoxicants originated from a singular principle that states;

"O you who believe! Approach not As-Salāt (the prayer) when you are in a drunken state until you know (the meaning) of what you utter..." - Qur'ān, 4:43

This emphasizes the importance of clarity in prayer recitations, which should be delivered with intention and proper wording. Therefore, mindfulness in prayer is essential—being fully aware of what you are saying.

Following this, the complete prohibition is articulated.

"O you who believe! Intoxicants (all kinds of alcoholic drinks), gambling, Al-Ansāb, and Al-Azlām (arrows for seeking luck

or decision) are an abomination of Shaitān's (Satan)
handiwork. So avoid (strictly all) that (abomination) in order
that you may be successful. Shaitān (Satan) wants only to
excite enmity and hatred between you with intoxicants
(alcoholic drinks) and gambling, and hinder you from the
remembrance of Allāh and from As-Salāt (the prayer). So, will
you not then abstain? – Qur'ān, 5:90-91

We see from this that intoxication can lead to increased
hostility and animosity among individuals while also hin-
dering their connection with God during prayer. It impairs
their God-given ability to reason clearly. Similarly, prayer
may be compromised when one is sleepy or lacks mindfulness. The Prophet Muhammad (PBUH) advised,

"If one of you is sleepy while praying, let him rest for a while so
that he can understand the meaning of what he is saying."[2]

This spotlights the importance of mental clarity for
success.

Our ability to observe is not solely affected by intoxication; it can also be diminished by overloading the mind
with concerns beyond our control. This is precisely why we
adhere to the principles of our chosen Creed—to guide us
in the right direction. Such principles help us stay focused,
allowing us to concentrate on what truly matters and enhancing our capacity to engage with our circumstances.

Following this path, we avoid speaking ill of others,
damaging their reputations, or slandering them. Adhering to these guidelines enables us to clear our own issues

---

[2] Sunan al-Tirmidhī, Hadīth No. 355

and become more effective in life. When we focus on our own shortcomings rather than meddling in others' affairs, we are better positioned for self-assessment. Conversations with friends should center around mutual growth and improvement rather than dwelling on absent individuals.

On the authority of Abū Hurayrah (R.A) who said: The Messenger of Allāh (PBUH) said,

"Part of the perfection of one's Islām is his leaving that which does not concern him."[3]

3. Reflection

The next step, following mindfulness and observation, is to engage in deep reflection—seriously considering what you have carefully observed. Intoxicants, as previously mentioned, often serve to trivialize the stark realities of life.

Living an unhealthy lifestyle can leave a person restless and anxious. Instead of taking the time to contemplate necessary changes, they may turn to alcohol or drugs as a temporary escape from the pain. Entertainment can serve a similar purpose, with phrases like *"dance and forget your sorrows"* woven into many popular songs. However, there is much to learn from those sorrows that could lead to a better life for them and society.

Mindfulness involves recognizing when a person is reaching for another drink, veering down a destructive

---

[3]Sunan al-Tirmidhī, Hadīth No. 2318, Ibn Mājah, Hadīth No. 3976

path. Observation means noticing the signs of addiction and the negative impact it has on their lives.

Reflection is about considering the preventable diseases that could stem from one's drinking. It means envisioning the long, lonely nights their partners might spend in a hospital corridor, the questions their children may ask about their unexplained absence or the deep regret they will feel as they lie motionless on a hospital bed, life slipping away. In those moments, they might curse the day they first turned to the bottle, fully aware that their lack of self-control led them to this dire situation, humbled to their knees by their own choices. The vivid imagery a person creates in their mind makes it easier to take the right actions and delay gratification.

In marriage, mindfulness means being aware of your behavior at home and how you represent your family in public. Being observant involves noticing the impact of your actions on your loved ones. Reflecting requires thinking critically about how your choices affect your immediate family.

For instance, if a man fails to provide for his wife, she may patiently take on a job, working multiple shifts. While she strives to support the family, her increased busyness may detract from her roles as a hands-on mother and devoted wife. The husband might then find himself admiring other women, questioning why his wife is not as amazing as they seem.

If he were more mindful, he might recognize that he has fallen short of his responsibilities as a provider. He could observe that his wife is merely trying to fill the gaps he has left, motivated by love and a desire to support him.

This realization might lead him to appreciate her efforts, acknowledging that her new job affects her ability to fulfill her primary roles at home. Instead of seeking comfort with another woman, he could reflect deeply on how to find a mutually beneficial solution.

Similarly, a married man might reconsider an affair with a mistress, recognizing that her allure lies in her availability and freedom from the responsibilities of motherhood. An attentive man will understand that true happiness comes from his wife's commitment and sacrifices. By reflecting on these truths, he may come around to see infidelity as a profound betrayal of the woman who has devoted her life to him.

The man who lacks awareness, driven by his lust, fixates only on physical appearances, eager for a fleeting moment of pleasure. This myopic view stems from his ignorance and inability to reflect on deeper consequences. He lives almost instinctively, like a base animal, unable to reconsider his choices, which lays the groundwork for numerous sinful actions.

Beginning with the issue of disbelief, Allāh states:

"Do they not reflect? There is no madness in their companion (Muhammad). He is but a plain warner." – Qur'ān, 7:184

This verse was revealed in response to the baseless accusations made by the chiefs of Makkah, who claimed that the Prophet Muhammad (PBUH) was deranged. These unfounded slurs came from those who knew him well, who had watched him grow up as a trustworthy individual without a hint of madness. Yet, they sought to discredit his sanity and, by extension, his message.

We see similar behavior today. When confronted with uncomfortable truths, many dismiss them with derogatory labels. Common tags include *"extremist,"* version of Islām, and *"extreme"* interpretation of the Shari'ah, among other slurs, used casually to dissuade seekers of truth.

A thoughtful person who pays attention tunes out the noise and closely investigates the message to uncover the supposed truth or, at the very least, satisfy their curiosity.

"(This is) a Book (the Qur'ān) which We have sent down to you, full of blessings that they may ponder over its Verses, and that men of understanding may remember." - Qur'ān, 38:29

The Islāmic term for a disbeliever is *"Kāfir,"* from *"Kufr"* derived from *"kafara,"* which means *"to conceal"* or *"to cover."* This term is likened to a farmer burying seeds in the ground. It describes someone who hides or obscures the truth, often by resisting the innate human ability for self-reflection and failing to sincerely contemplate what the truth might be. Fortunately, as promised, you will find the path to Ultimate Truth.

"There is no compulsion in religion. Verily, the Right Path has become distinct from the wrong path..." – Qur'ān, 2:256

We are inherently created with a *'fitrah,'* a natural disposition towards the Ultimate Truth regarding human existence and its connection to the Divine; all encapsulated in our Creed. The truth about the correct Creed is often clear; however, many hinder themselves—by their own evil machinations—from contemplating the true meaning of that truth with sincerity.

Many individuals refrain from reflecting on the signs around them. These signs serve only to benefit those on the straight path—those who pay careful attention, who are mindful enough to observe, and then reflect on what they see.

"... Verily, in this are signs for a people who think deeply." - Qur'ān, 39:42

If the Qur'ān had been authored by mere humans pretending to be divine, it would likely discourage the use of human intellect—however limited—in the pursuit of truth and deep reflection. It would have contained obvious inconsistencies and discouraged critical thinking, perhaps fearing that seekers of truth might be dissuaded by its lack of logic. Instead, the Qur'ān invites intellectual engagement with its verses, urging readers to contemplate them deeply.

"Do they not then think deeply in the Qur'ān, or are their hearts locked up (from understanding it)?" - Qur'ān, 47:24

4. Prioritization

Now that you have practiced mindfulness, observation, and reflection, it is time to reorganize your priorities. Drawing from previously used examples, you can recognize how your actions may harm your family's delicate fabric or jeopardize your health.

Do you genuinely want to love and protect your family, or will you succumb to fleeting pleasures that could cause them pain?

Would you prefer a harmonious family built on mutual love and respect or risk it all for a stranger?

A part of paying attention involves making informed choices based on your reflections. It requires direction, and you can only find that direction by letting go of harmful choices that conflict with your guiding principles.

Imagine you are driving on a straight road to a distant destination with just enough fuel to reach it. Your goal is a rewarding dinner waiting for you at the end. If you decide to stray from your path to feast on some not-so-nice meal momentarily, you might enjoy a brief distraction, but you risk running out of fuel and failing to reach your ultimate goal. Most people would choose to stay focused, knowing that a little patience will lead to greater rewards.

Consider someone who is mindful of their sugar intake and recognizes the dangers of overindulgence. They reflect on the potential suffering their habits might cause their family. Yet, they may continue down a detrimental path if they do not prioritize their family's well-being over fleeting enjoyment.

Interestingly, while priorities used to be singular, just one major priority, today, we often juggle multiple priorities, so the plural "priorities" has become more common. However, to maintain focus, one overarching priority—the 'Mother Priority'—must be identified, which should guide all others. This should be your Creed, rooted in your connection to the Divine, serving as what is called 'Mi'yār' or benchmark in Arabic for your decisions.

With this baseline, even if someone is unmindful or unaware of the consequences of their actions, prioritizing their Creed allows them to align their choices with the abiding edicts of the Qur'ān, hence keeping their actions within proper behavior. His mindfulness, observation, and reflection may also not always bring the desired results because he might be unaware of his biases. But, by prioritizing his Creed, he can dissect his conclusions and decisions, seeing if they agree with his elected Creed. He, by default, submits to that which he has prioritized once he is honest about his actions and their adherence to that Creed. If his Creed remains his top priority, all other decisions must align with it.

"Say (O Muhammad): "Verily, my Salāt (prayer), my sacrifice, my living, and my dying are for Allāh, the Lord of the 'Ālamīn (mankind, jinns[4] and all that exists)." - Qur'ān, 6:162

Islām offers a unique reward system. It promises not only eternal bliss in paradise, where the delights are tailored to satisfy all of humanity's insatiable desires—in a human worldly sense—but also a fulfilling life here on Earth. Following the teachings of Islām does not only grant access to success in the afterlife; it also enriches your present existence with ease and fulfillment, reflecting the true essence of living according to its principles.

Abū al-'Abbās 'Abdullah bin 'Abbās (R.A) reports that, "One day I was riding (a horse/camel) behind the Prophet, peace and blessings be upon him, when he said,

---

[4]The Quran describes jinns as spirits made of smokeless fire and are not bound by the laws of time or space. while they can see us, they are invisible to us and can shape-shift. They have many of the same capabilities as humans, including the ability to have families, make moral choices, and exercise free will

"Young man, I will teach you some words. Be mindful of Allāh,
and He will take care of you. Be mindful of Him, and you shall
find Him at your side. If you ask, ask of Allāh. If you need help,
seek it from Allāh. Know that if the whole world were to gather in
order to help you, they would not be able to help you except if
Allāh had written so. And if the whole world were to gather in
order to harm you, they would not harm you except if Allāh had
written so. The pens have been lifted, and the pages are dry."[5]

This narration offers several lessons, the most important being that maintaining a good relationship with Allāh
ensures His support, even in the everyday aspects of life.
An average Muslim understands that pleasing Allāh and
avoiding disobedience will cater to his earthly needs. However, this should not be mistaken for laziness or a lack
of effort in pursuing success. Recall the story of the man
whom the Prophet (PBUH) advised first to secure his camel
and then pray for its safety, highlighting the importance
of doing our part while at the same time relying on Allāh.[6]

The key point here is to be mindful enough to recognize
that while you may chase the fleeting allure of worldly
pursuits, the ultimate outcome—whether you achieve your
goals—lies with Allāh. It is essential to understand that
if results were solely determined by individual effort, the
hardest workers would always reap the greatest rewards.
Unfortunately, this is not always the case. Reflecting on
these realities reminds us that since the final results are
in Allāh's Hands, disobedience can nullify all our efforts.
Therefore, it is crucial to prioritize Him.

---

[5] Sunan al-Tirmidhī, Hadīth No. 2516
[6] Sunan Al-Tirmidhī, Hadīth No. 2517

"...And whosoever fears Allāh and keeps his duty to Him, He will make a way for him to get out (from every difficulty). And He will provide him from (sources) he never could imagine. And whosoever puts his trust in Allāh, then He will suffice him. Verily, Allāh will accomplish his purpose. Indeed Allāh has set a measure for all things." - Qur'ān, 65:2-3

This means you must uphold your end of the bargain by working hard and giving your utmost effort without wavering. When faced with the temptation to displease Allāh, prioritize Him—fulfill His Commands—because you ultimately recognize that only He can provide what you truly seek. The promise is clear: He will certainly make a way if you are mindful of Him. Conversely, the opposite holds true.

This principle also applies to anyone dissatisfied with their worldly status, income, or spouse. If you continue to seek Allāh's pleasure and refrain from His prohibitions, despite external pressures to compromise, Allāh promises to create a path to satisfaction, even when it seems unattainable.

03

A Weak Web, Strengthened
by Confusion

THE 29th chapter of the Qur'ān is intriguingly titled 'Al-Ankabūt,' which translates to 'The Spider.' This chapter begins with a discussion about the trials we face in this life.

"Do people think that they will be left alone because they say: 'We believe,' and will not be tested. We certainly tested those before them. And in this way Allah will clearly distinguish between those who are truthful and those who are liars." –
Qur'ān, 29:2-3

The theme of this chapter revolves around the fragile web of a spider. Given its weakness, one might wonder how such a delicate structure can trap larger insects. This serves as a metaphor: if you place your hopes in anything other than Allāh, your protection is, in fact, weak and vulnerable. From this, we can glean an important lesson: if you find yourself caught in the complex web of worldly affairs—its temptations, challenges, and tests—they are not as daunting as they may seem, especially when you genuinely rely on Allāh. Allāh says in verse 41 of the same chapter:

"The likeness of those who take Auliyā' (protectors and helpers) other than Allāh is as the likeness of a spider, who builds (for itself) a house, but verily, the frailest (weakest) of houses is the spider's house; if they but knew." – Qur'ān, 29:41

We find that the challenges that bind us and create confusion in our lives are indeed surmountable, particularly if we adhere to the Straight Path. The worldly trials you face may feel overwhelming, mentally taxing, and hard to comprehend, yet they can be navigated if you free yourself from the entanglements of worldly distractions and the snares of a mesh of webs. You can escape this fragile web by staying committed to the Straight Path and striving to remain steadfast. Allāh says in the final verse of this chapter:

"As for those who strive hard in Us (Our Cause), We will surely guide them to Our Paths (i.e. Allāh's Religion—Islāmic Monotheism). And verily, Allāh is with the Muhsinūn (good doers)." – Qur'ān, 29:69

A Practical Example

Consider someone who works tirelessly, driven by a desperate need to accumulate wealth. This person endures significant mental and physical strain yet may still not achieve their financial goals. Now, compare them to another individual who works hard and desires the same wealth but understands that only Allāh can provide it. This second person submits to Allāh's will, accepting that wealth is granted according to His perfect wisdom. When wealth comes, they are grateful; when it does not, they remain composed and patient, recognizing Allāh's justice. This perspective liberates them from the *"I must be rich"* mentality, giving them greater freedom and flexibility, knowing that after all their efforts, the ultimate outcome lies with a Higher Power that knows what is best for them. They are faithful!

Paying Attention to Trials

People often struggle to find meaning in the trials they face. It is said that *sometimes we feel buried, but in reality, we realize in the end we were being planted to sprout anew and attain greatness.* Islām exhorts us to pray against life's many tribulations. However, we are equally encouraged to keep our composure when life deals us a hurtful hand, understanding that, perhaps, this might be Allāh's way of emboldening our resolve, strengthening us through our pains, preparing us for future challenges, and teaching us valuable lessons, so things might get better for us when the dust does settle.

Perhaps, the trial draws us closer to Allāh, a sure path leading to ultimate good. Perhaps it might prepare us for a challenge ahead or to give us a good head start for something we might need later. It might teach us to empathize with others who are struggling. Or it might be a slap on the wrist—light punishment in the short term—for our indiscretions to prevent a greater punishment, or it might be to avert an incoming danger, or as a lesson to keep your feet strong, steadfast on the right path.

If we only focus on the trials themselves—without recognizing the accompanying lessons or potential blessings—they can seem overwhelming. This confusion can lead to misplaced anger and suspicion toward others, often resulting in damaging relationships. Many people mistakenly believe that a good person should not experience misfortune, leading to unfounded accusations against friends or family.[1]

To avoid confusion during such times, the Islāmic creed provides a clear framework for response:

- *"I may not understand why this is happening, but I recognize it as part of Allāh's decree."*

- *"Allāh is just; therefore, if I face loss, I can find greater reward in patience and learning from this experience."*

- *"There are many upsides to this painful situation, and even if I cannot momentarily see the immediate benefits in this world, there is an ultimate reward for me if I keep to the straight path, unwaveringly."*

---

[1] This is not in relation to the kind of harm people can directly afflict on you but rather other types of misfortunes that are beyond our control.

With this understanding, trials lose much of their weight. While they may appear daunting to those with weaker faith, strong conviction helps us view challenges for what they truly are: the weak webs of a spider that can barely hold a fly.

When we get trapped in the unrealistic web of expectations that life must be perfect, we invite confusion. This explains why many celebrities find themselves lost despite their fame and fortune—they discover that external success does not guarantee inner peace. What they truly need is a grounding in faith, which provides clarity and tranquility that wealth and status cannot.

That, in a nutshell, is the proper understanding of life and its many trials. A slight shift in your outlook—that everything happens for good—can help you keep some of the most distressing situations under control, helping you, by extension, to stay unjaded.

Pay Attention to Your Reactions to Negative Events

Our reactions to trials need not drive us into misery and distress if our reliance is solely on Allāh. For every challenge threatening to break our spirit, others in similar situations stand strong and composed. One way to gauge your resilience is to observe how steadfast you remain on the straight path and how diligently you adhere to your beliefs, as exemplified in divine teachings. Allāh says:

"...then whoever follows My Guidance shall neither go astray, nor fall into distress and misery. But whosoever turns away from My Reminder (i.e. neither believes in this Qur'ān nor acts on its orders, etc.) verily, for him is a life of hardship..." -

Qur'ān, 20:123-124

*Are you quick to stray from the principles of your faith just
because of a challenging situation?*

Such a reaction only adds to your confusion and misfortune. As earlier verses remind us, anything we rely on
other than Allāh is ultimately weak by default, even if we
do not realize it. If you depend on Allāh, you will always
find Him sufficient.

Ask yourself:

*If you desire something that seems out of reach through
permissible means, do you think you can bypass Allāh's will? Are
you not aware that nothing happens without His permission? If
you understand this, why disobey Him?*

Your readiness to turn to disobedience in tough times
raises questions about your belief in Allāh as the Lord of
the Worlds, worthy of your exclusive worship.

Today's economy is filled with interest-based and un-
ethical practices. Some claim, "You cannot succeed in
business without engaging in these practices." Such statements undermine our faith that Allāh's guidance should
lead our lives and that He is capable of all things. Believing
there is no way out except to compromise shows a fundamental misunderstanding of our knowledge about Allāh
and a lack of awareness of the consequences of our actions.

A Muslim shop owner who thinks playing popular music with vulgar lyrics is necessary to attract customers.
Similarly, a Muslim fashion designer may feel compelled

to showcase revealing outfits to boost sales. Such justifications for forbidden actions call into question one's faith that true wealth comes solely from Allāh.

A Muslim must adhere to what is permissible, even if the impermissible seems necessary for success. Failures along the way are merely tests with set durations. Even if they last a lifetime, remember that this worldly life pales in comparison to the hereafter, where trials endured in this life will yield lasting benefits.

The moral decay within affluent communities, where youth often resort to fraud and illegal possession of drugs and guns to achieve a superficial sense of success and momentary pleasure, is marked by luxury possessions and excess wealth. This lifestyle raises questions about the legitimacy of their gains and whether such wealth can be divinely sanctioned. To the ignorant mind, while these fraudulent activities might seem to benefit the local economy by stimulating trade and services, the deeper implications reveal a troubling reality: prioritizing material wealth over spiritual integrity can lead to catastrophic consequences, including violence, tragedy, and injustice.

Ultimately, what may appear to the ignorant as a harmless or even beneficial practice—fraud and illegal possession—harbors destructive effects on both individuals and society. The fallout includes increased crime, loss of innocent lives, and unjust punishment of those wrongfully accused. This serves as a stark reminder that deceitful actions, even if they momentarily enrich certain members of the community, undermine the moral fabric of society and lead to dire repercussions for all.

"Corruption has spread on land and sea as a result of what people's hands have done, so that Allāh may cause them to taste the consequences of some of their deeds and perhaps they might return to the Right Path" - Qur'ān, 30:41

We should avoid the mindset that being on the straight path has not improved our situation. Instead, we must practice patience and continue on our path until we gain greater clarity and understanding of Allāh's plans for us.

"O my son! Aqim-is-Salāt (perform As-Salāt), enjoin (people) for Al–Ma'rūf (Islāmic Monotheism and all that is good), and forbid (people) from Al–Munkar (i.e. disbelief in the Oneness of Allāh, polytheism of all kinds and all that is evil and bad), and bear with patience whatever befall you. Verily! These are some of the important commandments ordered by Allāh with no exemption." - Qur'ān, 31:17

One of the main ideas we can deduce from this verse is that Allāh sheds light on the importance of being patient on the straight path while firmly adhering to His commands. Allāh placed His Prophets in situations that demonstrated their remarkable patience—an example for us to follow—even though He was fully aware of their unwavering faith and determination.

"And many a Prophet (i.e. many from amongst the Prophets) fought (in Allāh's Cause) and along with him (fought) large bands of religious learned men. But they never lost heart for that which did befall them in Allāh's Way, nor did they weaken nor degrade themselves. And Allāh loves As-Sābirīn (the patient ones, etc.)." - Qur'ān, 3:146

He also, in the same breadth, outlines the appropriate behavior we should exhibit when faced with calamity, reminding us that His tests are a guaranteed part of life.

"And certainly, We shall test you with something of fear, hunger, loss of wealth, lives and fruits, but give glad tidings to As-Sabirīn (the patient ones, etc.). Who, when afflicted with calamity, say: "Truly! To Allāh we belong and truly, to Him we shall return." They are those on whom are the Salawāt (i.e. blessings, etc.) (i.e. who are blessed and will be forgiven) from their Lord, and (they are those who) receive His Mercy, and it is they who are the guided-ones." - Qur'ān, 2:155-157

In addition to adhering to what is permissible, it is crucial to pay attention to your reaction when calamity strikes—specifically, your level of patience. This means not just enduring despair with the mindset of *"there is nothing I can do"* but demonstrating patience right from the moment the hardship begins. As the Prophet (PBUH) said,

"Patience is at the first stroke of calamity,"[2]

One way to assess your commitment to the straight path is by observing your initial reaction to challenging or unsettling situations. When you place your complete trust in Allāh, your first response should be one of submission to His decree, characterized by patience and calmness in the face of adversity. This patience stems from a mindset that says,

---

[2] Ṣaḥīḥ al-Bukhārī, Hadīth No. 1302 and Ṣaḥīḥ Muslim, Hadīth No. 926

"I have submitted to Allāh; my trust in Him is unwavering, and I believe that, in the long run, everything will work in my favor as long as I remain consistent in my submission."

There is a story of a Shaykh (Islāmic Scholar) who was interrupted during a lecture by a messenger who informed him that his ship, carrying all his wealth in merchandise, had capsized at sea. The Shaykh paused, said *"Alhamdulillāh,"*[3] and continued his lecture, seemingly unfazed and poised as if nothing had happened. Shortly after, another messenger arrived with the news that the ship had not sunk and that all was intact. Again, the Shaykh paused, said *"Alhamdulillāh,"* and resumed teaching.

When his students inquired about his remarkable composure in both instances—first in loss and then in restoration—the Shaykh explained that his contentment and reliance on Allāh's equitable Will were the common threads. Whether facing gain or loss, his heart remained steadfast in gratitude, recognizing that everything comes from and returns to Him.

Paying Attention to Priority

From the previous chapter, we recall that the term *"priority"* has evolved from a singular concept to the plural *"priorities,"* a distracting pile of "important" things. Your priority should be the central focus that encompasses and addresses life's most critical aspects. What could be more vital than your faith in the Divine? Your Creed—the Straight Path—guides all areas of your life.

---

[3] Meaning Praise be to Allāh

Many of the challenges we worry about would be resolved or diminished if we strengthened our relationship with Allāh. Even when these challenges arise, we can find solace in the consolation that Allāh knows best. This is emphasized by the Prophet Muhammad (PBUH) when he said,

"How wonderful the affair of the believer is! Indeed, all of his affairs are good for him. This is for no one but the believer. If something good happens to him, he is grateful to Allāh, which is good for him. And if something bad happens to him, he has patience, which is good for him."[4]

This means that everything will fall into place if we prioritize our faith, making Islām the ultimate focus in our lives—the singular priority that influences everything else.

Consider a situation where a business deal falls through or you struggle with settling down with a partner and starting a family. In such times, you might find yourself praying earnestly for these outcomes.

But have you considered that you might be addressing the wrong issue?

When tragedy strikes, it is common for the affected to seek help from others to help intensify prayers on their behalf. However, if we turn inward and reflect, we may realize that we are falling short of our obligations to Allāh. Such shortcomings often require personal introspection and rectification rather than reliance on a third party.

---

[4] Ṣaḥīḥ Muslim, Hadīth No. 2999

When faced with difficulties, ensure you have not severed your connection with the Source—Allāh. This is not to say that problems are not inherent in human existence; they are like the obstacles one encounters in a race.

As mentioned earlier, everyone will face trials. However, it is essential to first examine yourself, checking for possible gaps or lapses in your relationship with Allāh is a starting point in understanding your unique situation. Once you confirm that you are still striving to remain on the straight path, you can pray and remain hopeful, knowing you are not standing in the way of your own solutions. If the problem persists, take solace in the fact that your perseverance may be rewarded. It may also be that Allāh intends to elevate your spiritual standing, drawing you closer through these trials. Perhaps you have been consistent with your five daily prayers but neglected the midnight prayers; this challenge could serve as a wake-up call, urging you to deepen your spiritual commitment.

Indeed, sometimes our disobedience to Allāh can lead to challenges in our lives that we might not see as connected. As Allāh says regarding the punishment of the people of Egypt during the time of Moses:

"And indeed We punished the people of Fir'aun (Pharaoh) with years of drought and shortness of fruits (crops, etc.), that they might remember (take heed)." - Qur'ān, 7:130

This suggests that Allāh may impose punishment as a consequence of a transgression, such as straying from the straight path.

Imagine a scenario where someone falls asleep while driving, and another driver trailing behind sees them heading toward a ditch. It would be entirely reasonable for that driver to gently nudge the sleeping driver to alert them of the impending danger, potentially saving their life. In this context, we would likely be grateful for the intervention, focusing more on the danger averted than the minor dent to the car. Now, what if that savior was also the one who purchased the car for you? Then the situation becomes even more trivial.

However, two questions may arise:

First, why does not Allāh simply wake the driver up, given His absolute power to do so?

Second, what about those who engage in wrongdoing yet seem to achieve their desires without consequence?

Regarding Allāh's ability to awaken the driver, the straight-forward answer is that sometimes the process itself is necessary for growth. If Allāh were to rouse every drowsy driver, people might become complacent, no longer taking the responsibility to stay alert. Furthermore, He has granted us free will, which is essential in our choices.

As for those who cheat and appear to "get away with it," they are ultimately at a disadvantage. Their fleeting gains will likely lead them further away from the straight path.

The question of why Allāh delays punishment for wrong-doing, even when immediate consequences might prompt a change, is also significant. Immediate retribution is not a universal favor; it usually serves as a guiding light for some to redirect them toward Allāh. Thus, we should be thankful when a punishment serves to bring us back home. Allāh desires what is best for us, but not everyone is deserving of this mercy.

If the driver heading for the ditch had previously harmed an innocent child without remorse, people would likely feel no obligation to warn him. Allāh knows the unseen and the hidden sins of those who remain unpunished, and sometimes He allows them to stray further as a means to prepare them for greater consequences in the hereafter.

"And if Allāh were to punish men for that which they earned, He would not leave a moving (living) creature on the surface of the earth, but He gives them respite to an appointed term, and when their term comes, then verily, Allāh is Ever All-Seer of His slaves." - Qur'ān 35:45

From this verse, we learn that all of humanity[5] has sinned and would face just retribution if not for Allāh's boundless mercy. He also states:

"And were Allāh to hasten for mankind the evil (they invoke for themselves and for their children, etc. while in a state of anger) as He hastens for them the good (they invoke) then they would have been ruined. So We leave those who expect not their meeting with Us, in their trespasses, wandering blindly in distraction." - Qur'ān, 10:11

Now, we can understand that Allāh may delay certain punishments, allowing the wicked to continue in their wrongdoings, causing them to stray even further from His path.

Can you now see how a true believer may face calamity yet remain grateful to Allāh?

---

[5] Excluding children who are yet to attain puberty and unable to distinguish right from wrong

It is clear how such trials can actually be a favor from Allāh to His beloved servant. Saʿd ibn Abī Waqqās reported: I said, "O Messenger of Allāh, which people are tested most severely?" The Messenger of Allāh,(PBUH), said,

"They are the prophets, then the next best, then the next best. A man is put to trial according to his religion. If he is firm in his religion, his trials will be more severe. If he is weak in his religion, he is put to trial according to his strength in religion. The servant will continue to be put to trial until he is left walking upon the earth without any sin."[6]

Once you make Islām your priority and consistently ensure you have not strayed from the path, your affairs will be well-managed, regardless of life's challenges.

When Islām is your focus, consider how your rank in the hereafter may have risen, even if it appears diminished in this world. You may be aging without children, but this has allowed you the opportunity to engage in night prayers. You may be facing poverty, yet this hardship has cultivated your patience. As the Prophet (PBUH) said, the reward for patience is paradise.

Have you truly gained less than the impatient, miserly rich person who possesses great wealth?

Not when Islām is your priority.

Prioritizing Islām helps us concentrate on what truly matters, transforming the negatives in your life into positives. It reassures us that trials can lead to eternal reward, enhancing our spiritual standing rather than merely reflecting our sins. The narratives of Allāh's Prophets are

---

[6]Sunan al-Tirmidhī, Hadīth No. 2398 and Sunan Ibn Mājah, Hadīth No. 4023

filled with examples of their numerous trials—experiences we might not expect to encounter today.

a person may wish to lament their lack of children, yet consider the Prophet Ibrahim (Abraham, PBUH), whom Allāh describes as *"...an Ummah (a leader having all the good righteous qualities), or a nation, obedient to Allāh, Hanīfa (i.e. to worship none but Allāh), and he was not one of those who were Al-Mushrikūn (polytheists, idolaters, disbelievers in the Oneness of Allāh, and those who joined partners with Allāh)"*[7] remained childless well into his old age. When he prayed for a worthy progeny, he thoughtfully specified the qualities he desired, reflecting his priorities in life. He said, *"My Lord! Grant me (offspring) from the righteous."*[8]

When he finally had a child, he was commanded to sacrifice him to Allāh. This was a grueling test, yet he did not waver; he stood strong, ready to fulfill the Divine command. Clearly, his priority was not fatherhood but submission to Allāh's Will in Islām—the very reason he sought a righteous child in the first place.

All of the noble Prophet Muhammad's (PBUH) children died during his lifetime, except for one, his daughter Fātimah. In contrast, many today may never experience the pain of burying a child. Yet, they feel cursed and unlucky due to their struggles, lost in confusion born from shallow thinking, rethreading and strengthening, by their corrupted thinking, the spider's web in which they are trapped.

---

[7] Qur'ān, 16:120
[8] Qur'ān, 37:100

04

Our Ultimate Desire

W*HAT if life is not really as complex as we think?*

What if all our problems can be traced to a singular primary cause, where all our problems are interconnected, so much so that if we found the cause, all of these problems could effectively be resolved?

Everyone faces unique trials and challenges, but some individuals find security within themselves by fully understanding their difficulties and leveraging them to gain something better than what was lost. Such a person will always find a way through. Indeed, there is always a way out of every difficulty for those who are in harmony with God.

"...And whosoever fears Allāh and keeps his duty to Him, He will make a way for him to get out (from every difficulty). And He will provide him from (sources) he never could imagine. And whosoever puts his trust in Allāh, then He will suffice him. Verily, Allāh will accomplish his purpose. Indeed Allāh has set a measure for all things." - Qur'ān, 65:2-3

From the above verse, we see Allāh's promise that He will surely provide a way for us if we are mindful of Him, remain dutiful, and place our utmost trust in Him. You might want to reflect on whether that persistent problem or seemingly insurmountable misfortune remains unresolved due to your negligence or a lack of God-consciousness, distancing you from Allāh's promise.

There is a concept known as a Catalyst Solution—this master solution addresses the core issue, resolving everything else. Having the consciousness of Allāh, being dutiful to Him, and placing our trust in Him exemplifies the peak of this principle. It is a Catalyst Solution to many other ailments and calamities that may befall us.

Many of us misinterpret our challenges, mislabeling them. In truth, most problems can be distilled down to our pursuit of happiness. We all seek tranquility—the genuine sense of peace that fills our minds and hearts.

We desire money because it promises relief from the overwhelming demands and endless desires that disrupt our peace. We seek security to alleviate fear, which disturbs our calm. We strive to expand our influence to tackle the challenges that unsettle us, and the list goes on.

So, what is Peace of Mind?

Peace of Mind – The Inner Calm

When people say that being wealthy is not solely about having money, they are often met with skepticism and the claim that *"money solves all problems"* or as we say in Nigeria, *"money stops nonsense."* While money can indeed provide an outward appearance of success and power if it does not bring peace of mind, its purpose is ultimately defeated. Consider the correlation between rich, famous celebrities and the rising rates of suicide among them. Money and fame did not provide them with that sense of peace. What we truly seek is peace of mind, inner calm, and tranquility.

A man might be the richest in the world but remain anxious about maintaining his wealth, while another, not on any rich list, may find peace without the burden of such concerns. If the wealthiest man is assured that nothing could take away his status, his distress might diminish. This illustrates that the true goal of acquiring wealth is to ensure nothing disrupts our inner calm. Thus, the ultimate aim of the wealthiest individual might be easily realized by someone with far less.

This is why wealth can be a burden for some. As Allāh says,

"So let not their wealth or their children amaze you (O Muhammad); in reality, Allāh's Plan is to punish them with these things in the life of the this world, and that their souls shall depart (die) while they are disbelievers." - Qur'ān, 9:55

Additionally, the aspirations of the wealthiest man may be unattainable. He seeks to secure his status as the richest forever—a goal that is fundamentally impossible. Consequently, he finds himself in a precarious position, even while a multitude admires his outward possessions and apparent charm.

With regard to our perpetual accumulation and pursuit of wealth, true inner peace is best achieved through contentment with less, as human desires are limitless and insatiable. This is why the Prophet (PBUH) said,

"If the son of Adam had two valleys of gold, he would wish for a third, for nothing can fill the belly of Adam's son except dust. And Allāh forgives him who repents to Him."[1]

Cyclical competition in the pursuit of wealth often disrupts peace of mind, as it ties your sense of calm to achieving this worldly success. By setting attainable goals, you increase your chances of reaching them and finding that peace. The Prophet (PBUH) also said,

"Verily, it is not poverty that I fear for you, but I fear that the world will be spread out before you, as it was spread out before those who came before you, and you will compete for it as they competed for it, and it will destroy you as it destroyed them."[2]

There certainly is no peace of mind without taming our yearnings for the things of this fleeting world. This should not be mistaken for a discouragement to healthy striving; it is to help tailor your desires. Perhaps the most beneficial way of striving towards achieving our goals is believing in Predestinations—Destiny. So, we toil hard but temper our periodic failures in the contentment that whatever was written for us will never miss us. Remember how Belief in

[1] Ṣaḥīḥ Bukhārī, Hadīth No. 6439, Ṣaḥīḥ Muslim, Hadīth No. 1048
[2] Ṣaḥīḥ Bukhārī, Hadīth No. 3158, Ṣaḥīḥ Muslim, Hadīth No. 2961

Destiny is one of the articles of our Foundational Creed? It all comes together now. With this understanding that all of our affairs are predestined, we are able to control our excessive desires for wealth, starving them of unmerited focus. The Prophet (PBUH) said,

"Whoever is focused only on this world, Allāh will confound his affairs and make him fear poverty constantly, and he will not get anything of this world except that which has been decreed for him. Whoever is focused on the Hereafter, Allāh will settle his affairs for him and make him feel content with his lot, and his provision and worldly gains will undoubtedly come to him."[3]

Another guideline for pursuing wealth was established by the Prophet (PBUH) when he said

"Jibrīl (Gabriel) inspired to me that no soul will die until it has completed its allotted time span and received its provision in full. So be moderate in seeking provision, and no one of you should let thinking that provision is slow in coming prompt him to seek it by sinful means, for what is with Allāh cannot be attained except through obedience to Him"[4]

However, Inner Peace is not sought through wealth alone. There are other desires, like having children, seeking status, and yearning for momentary pleasures, as seen in the realms of love and our social need for acceptance. Without clearly defining our desires, we may never find true peace. A person may long for children yet remain at

---

[3] Sunan Ibn Mājah, Hadīth No. 4105
[4] Sunan Ibn Mājah, Hadīth No. 2144

peace with the understanding that, despite their efforts, not everyone will be blessed with offspring.

"To Allāh belongs the kingdom of the heavens and the earth. He creates what He wills. He bestows female (offspring) upon whom He wills, and bestows male (offspring) upon whom He wills. Or He bestows both males and females, and He renders barren whom He wills. Verily, He is the All-Knower and is Able to do all things." - Qur'ān, 42:49-50

That simple realization shapes your expectations when you have children, fostering gratitude in your heart. Unfortunately, some beliefs hold that God's plans for people's lives are confined to what humans—limited by time and space—deem good. This perspective is inaccurate and can leave many in a constant state of anxiety, chasing the unattainable and struggling to find peace of mind despite their efforts

You may yearn for societal status, but there will always be those ranked higher than you. Even if you reach the highest office, the thought of someone more charismatic or wealthy who once held that position may linger in your mind. You might govern a great kingdom yet still feel uneasy knowing that throughout history, there have been kingdoms far greater and more prosperous than your own. Even if your kingdom is the greatest today so far, anxieties about future generations surpassing your achievements may arise.

Ultimately, few will attain outstanding status in this world. This emphasizes the restless nature of the mind when driven by desires for the fleeting allure of wealth and status. To find peace, we must not make the pursuit of societal status our ultimate goal, as this is a futile endeavor. Instead, we should focus on the higher aim: attaining the greatest rank in righteousness before our Creator, who reminds us:

"O mankind! We have created you from a male and a female, and made you into nations and tribes, that you may know one another. Verily, the most honorable of you with Allāh is that (believer) who has At-Taqwā [i.e., one of the Muttaqūn (pious – see V.2:2)]. Verily, Allāh is All-Knowing, All-Aware." – Qur'ān, 49:13

Allāh promises to elevate the status of the believers, above the unbelievers, when He said,

"Beautified is the life of this world for those who disbelieve, and they mock at those who believe. But those who obey Allāh's Orders and keep away from what He has forbidden will be above them on the Day of Resurrection. And Allāh gives (of His Bounty, Blessings, Favors, Honors, etc. on the Day of Resurrection) to whom He wills without limit." - Qur'ān, 2:212

It becomes clear and unmissable that the highest of all worldly statuses and achievements hold no value compared to the reward in the Hereafter A believer may achieve the highest rank in the hereafter through righteous deeds, allowing them to find peace of mind. Anything they receive in this world is merely a bonus—a gift that deepens their appreciation for their Lord and Creator. Moreover, their steadfast belief holds great significance even in this material life. This is reflected in the verse that shows Allāh grants a higher status to those who do good deeds, rather than to those who seek fame and wealth. As the Prophet (PBUH) says,

"Charity does not decrease wealth, no one forgives another except that Allāh increases his honor, and no one humbles himself for the sake of Allāh except that Allāh raises his status"[5]

When a Muslim practices humility and forgiveness towards others, he may feel that his status before Allāh has risen, bringing him a deep sense of peace. Similarly, when he gives in charity, he experiences fulfillment, sensing an increase in his true wealth rather than a decrease. The Prophet's wife, Aisha (R.A), narrated that they had slaughtered a sheep, and the Prophet (PBUH) asked, "What remains of it?" she replied, "Nothing remains of it, except its shoulders" The Prophet (PBUH) retorted, "All of it remains except its shoulders."[6] This means that what we give in charity represents what is truly ours and holds real value.

In contrast, many people chase after wealth, numerous friends, and external accomplishments to feel fulfilled. However, the believer finds a more direct path to happiness and inner peace through acts of kindness and generosity.

What about the desire to fully enjoy life?

The reason this enjoyment may feel inadequate for some is that it is inherently fleeting and comes with an expiration date. It is clear that in pursuing pleasure, we may find lasting peace of mind elusive in the long run. Much

---

[5] Ṣaḥīḥ Muslim, Hadīth No. 2588
[6] Sunan al-Tirmidhī, Hadīth No. 2470

has been said about delayed gratification—the practice of postponing immediate pleasure for a future benefit, effectively resisting the urge for a quick dopamine rush. However, in some faiths, certain desires are abandoned and demonized—exemplified by celibacy—not because they might be fulfilled later. In contrast, Islām encourages Muslims to appreciate and enjoy the various pleasures of this world while also recognizing that certain desires should be reserved for the Hereafter.

Even disbelievers in the Islāmic faith who recognize the principle of Karma understand that negative actions have repercussions. If your only sources of pleasure stem from harmful actions, you may find yourself grappling with discontent as genuine peace remains elusive. For example, a man who has sexual relations with his wife is happy when the result is pregnancy, while an adulterer experiences little satisfaction from a likely unacknowledged child, knowing the dire consequences of his actions.

Another source of inner turmoil arises from our innate desire for love and acceptance. As social beings, feeling accepted brings safety, which in turn fosters tranquility. Many of our personal pursuits revolve around seeking love and validation from others.

Islām, however, redirects this desire, urging us to place our Creator at the center of our affection. This divine love should take precedence over all others, guiding and regulating our relationships with those around us.

"And of mankind are some who take (for worship) others besides Allāh as rivals (to Allāh). They love them as they love Allāh. But those who believe, love Allāh more (than anything

else)..." - Qur'ān, 2:165

"Say (O Muhammad to mankind): "If you (really) love Allāh then follow me (i.e. accept Islāmic Monotheism, follow the Qur'ān and the Sunnah), Allāh will love you and forgive you of your sins. And Allāh is Oft-Forgiving, Most Merciful." - Qur'ān, 3:31

Here, we understand that a believer must prioritize their love for Allāh above all else. In return, we should harbor no misgivings about His reciprocity in care and love, as He promised. This love is manifested through our commitment to His commands and our adherence to the teachings of His Messenger, the Prophet Muhammad (PBUH).

When we cultivate a strong bond with our Creator, we become less reliant on seeking love from others. We can trust in His unwavering care and love, as He has promised that He is more than adept at expressing and showing this love. He extends this mutual love to encompass the community of believers, creating an unbreakable bond of support and connection. As the Prophet (PBUH) said,

"Whoever possesses the following three qualities will have the sweetness (delight) of faith: The one to whom Allāh and His Messenger become dearer than anything else; who loves a person, and he loves him only for Allāh's sake; who hates to revert to disbelief (atheism) as he hates to be thrown into the fire."[7]

The resulting community is united by genuine love that is built on a solid foundation. Their common thread

---

[7] Ṣaḥīḥ Bukhārī, Hadīth No. 16 and Ṣaḥīḥ Muslim, Hadīth No. 43

is the love of Allāh, accompanied by a mutual affection for everyone in the wider Ummah, or Muslim community. Simply by being a Muslim, you are embraced by a network of over 2 billion fellow believers who are bound to love you. This love and acceptance stems from shared values and a common belief system.

In summary, your understanding that life is not solely about accumulating wealth, along with your belief in pre-destination, recognizing that some may never have children, for instance, helps temper your desires. You realize that spiritual status in the hereafter far outweighs any material gains. Your love for Allāh and the love you receive in return all point to the undeniable truth:

when your focus is on Allāh, you will ultimately find peace of mind.

"Those who believe (in the Oneness of Allāh – Islāmic Monotheism), and whose hearts find rest in the remembrance of Allāh, Verily, in the remembrance of Allāh do hearts find rest." – Qur'ān, 13:28

Practical Steps to Achieving Peace of Mind

Psychologists have invested significant time and effort into exploring various avenues for achieving peace of mind, and interestingly, many of their findings align closely with Islāmic teachings. Here are six key insights and how adhering to the straight path can lead to them:

1. Accept What You Cannot Control

The essence of this principle is straightforward: *if you cannot change a situation, learn to accept it.* Many aspects of life are beyond our immediate control, and our worries can persist unless we surrender our struggles to a Higher Power. Islām teaches us that certain events in our lives are predetermined and will unfold as destined, regardless of our efforts to resist or alter them. Embracing this reality fosters inner peace and reduces anxiety.

> *"No calamity befalls on the earth or in yourselves but is inscribed in the Book of Decrees (Al-Lauh Al-Mahfūz), before We bring it into existence. Verily, that is easy for Allāh."* -
> Qur'ān, 57:22

And the Prophet (PBUH) said,

> *"There is no changing the divine decree except by supplication, and no one increases their lifespan except by good deeds"*[8]

A Muslim recognizes that certain life events are predetermined, some perceived as beneficial and others as challenging, each shaping his personal journey. This understanding facilitates acceptance of what is beyond his control, aligning with his faith, for which they will be rewarded.

2. Practice Forgiveness

Much has been written about the importance of forgiving yourself and others. This is crucial because holding

---

[8] Sunan Ibn Mājah, Hadīth No. 90

grudges creates negative energy that disrupts inner peace. Bitterness cannot coexist with tranquility. Forgiveness lightens our emotional burden. Bob Enright, a pioneer in the study of forgiveness at the University of Wisconsin-Madison, noted that true forgiveness involves offering something positive—empathy, compassion, and understanding—to those who have hurt us.

This transformative approach elevates forgiveness to a virtue and a powerful tool in positive psychology. Remarkably, the Qur'ān emphasized the value of forgiveness over 1,400 years ago, stating:

"The good deed and the evil deed cannot be equal. Repel (the evil) with one which is better, then verily! he, between whom and you there was enmity, (will become) as though he was a close friend." - Qur'ān, 41:34

This verse highlights not only the importance of forgiveness but also the value of responding to wrongdoing with kindness. Such gestures can lead to unexpected outcomes, transforming enmity into genuine friendship. Abū Ayyūb Al-Ansārī reported that the Prophet (PBUH) said,

"It is not lawful for a Muslim to abandon his (Muslim) brother beyond three nights; they meet so each turns away from the other, and the better of the two is the one who greets the other first."[9]

We can only envision how embodying the principle of being the bigger person, as encouraged by this verse and Hadīth, can bring tranquility to the do-gooder's soul

---

[9] Ṣaḥīḥ al-Bukhārī, Hadīth No. 6237

when relationships are mended. It is equally forbidden for a believer to despair of Allāh's mercy or lose hope in His forgiveness.

"Say: "O 'Ibādi (My slaves) who have transgressed against themselves (by committing evil deeds and sins)! Despair not of the Mercy of Allāh, verily Allāh forgives all sins. Truly, He is Oft-Forgiving, Most Merciful." - Qur'ān, 39:53

Forgiveness can also lighten the weight of sin. The Prophet (PBUH) said,

"Be merciful to others, and you will receive mercy. Forgive others and Allāh will forgive you."[10]

And he (PBUH) also said,

"Whoever suffers an injury and forgives [the person responsible], Allāh will raise his status to a higher degree and remove one of his sins."[11]

3./4. Practice Mindfulness/Make Time for Yourself

Mindfulness is often emphasized as a pathway to inner peace, requiring us to be fully present in each moment. As discussed in previous chapters, we have explored various ways to cultivate mindfulness. Many psychologists recommend meditation and moments of self-reflection. Fortunately, these practices are already integral to Islāmic life. Muslims are not only encouraged to reflect and introspect on the Qur'ān but they are also required to engage

---

[10] Sunan Abū Dawūd, Hadīth No. 4941
[11] Sunan Ibn Mājah, Hadīth No. 2693

in five daily prayers. These prayers include moments of silence, recitation, and introspective listening, both in congregation and individually.

In the Islāmic tradition, the practice of 'I'tikāf'—seclusion to withdraw from the distractions of life—holds great significance. This time is spent in a mosque and is dedicated to self-reflection and worship. Historically, just before the revelations of Islām, the Prophet Muhammad (PBUH) would retreat to the Cave of *Hirā* to reflect on the wonders of creation and the injustices of the pagan society of 7th-century Arabia. Islām has placed great importance on mindfulness; it says, *"Actions are to be judged by intention."*[12] This means that the believer must ensure his intentions match his good actions; only then can they be deemed acceptable. This, here, is the greatest call to mindfulness, as it juxtaposes the quality of an action with its respective intention. Profound, so much that Islām does not reckon as good an action undertaken with bad intentions.

In Islām, there is a further extension of mere mindfulness, elevated to the mindfulness of Allāh Himself. For He is fully aware of all our actions. This is foundational to solving many of our problems. The Prophet of Islām once advised a young man saying,

"Be mindful of God, and He will care for you. Be mindful of Him, and you shall find Him at your side...."[13]

---

[12] Ṣaḥīḥ al-Bukhārī, Ḥadīth No. 1, Ṣaḥīḥ Muslim, Ḥadīth No. 1907
[13] Sunan al-Tirmidhī, Ḥadīth No. 2516

5. Keep a Journal

Another widely recommended practice among psychologists studying peace of mind is keeping a journal. This habit allows for moments of reflection on daily experiences, capturing both highs and lows, as well as good fortunes and misfortunes. It encourages intentional thinking, helping many who may otherwise live on autopilot to engage in mindfulness. Journaling can serve as a tool for self-evaluation and personal growth.

The Qur'an also emphasizes the importance of reflecting on our lives when it says,

"O you who believe! Fear Allāh and keep your duty to Him. And let every person look to what he has sent forth for the morrow, and fear Allāh. Verily, Allāh is All-Aware of what you do." - Qur'ān, 59:18

The Prophet Muhammad (PBUH) was known to regularly reflect on his actions, often stating,

"By Allāh, I seek forgiveness from Allāh and repent to Him more than seventy times in a day."[14]

Umar Ibn al-Khattab (RadiyAllāhu 'anhu), a close companion of the Prophet (PBUH), also said,

"Hold yourself accountable before you are held accountable and weigh your deeds before they are weighed for you. It will be easy for you tomorrow (i.e., the Day of Judgment) should you evaluate

---

[14] Ṣaḥīḥ Bukhārī, Ḥadīth No. 6307

yourself today and be prepared for the great assembly on a Day when all things will be revealed and nothing will be hidden."[15]

Thus, we see that the practice of journaling, which psychologists recommend for self-reflection, is already embedded in Islāmic teachings. Muslims can use journaling to keep track of their deeds.

6. Reconnect with Nature

Finally, experts in psychology highlight the significance of nature. Numerous studies have demonstrated that time spent in natural settings can reduce emotional distress and foster inner peace. This connection to nature does not only alleviate anxiety and depression but it also enhances mindfulness and focus. Islām teaches that humanity has an intrinsic bond with nature, and one of the Devil's strategies is to disrupt this natural connection.

"... indeed I will order them to change the nature created by Allāh..." - Qur'ān, 4:119

To provide examples for our reflection, Allāh speaks of the perfect order inherent in nature, which He designed from the beginning. He states, in one instance,

"Do they not see the birds held (flying) in the midst of the sky? None holds them but Allāh. Verily, in this are clear proofs and signs for people who believe (in the Oneness of Allāh)." - Qur'ān, 16:79

---

[15] Al-Zuhd by Imām Ahmad (633) and Muḥa̅sabat al-Nafs of Al-Imām Ibn Abi al-Dunya, 2

Some scholars of Islām often agree that spending time in nature and reflecting on what Allāh has created in this universe, and seeing that as proof of the greatness and might of Allāh, is an act of worship that increases one's faith and certainty.[16] This is supported by numerous verses throughout the Qur'ān. Allāh says,

"Say: 'Travel in the land and see how (Allāh) originated creation, and then Allāh will bring forth (resurrect) the creation of the Hereafter (i.e. resurrection after death). Verily, Allāh is Able to do all things.'" - Qur'ān, 29:20

And He also said,

"Do they not look at the camels, how they are created? And at the heaven, how it is raised? And at the mountains, how they are rooted and fixed firm? And at the earth, how it is spread out?" - Qur'ān, 88:17-20

In another verse, Allāh describes those who reflect on nature as individuals of reason and deep intellect.

"Verily! In the creation of the heavens and the earth, and in the alternation of night and day, there are indeed signs for men of understanding. Those who remember Allāh (always, and in prayers) standing, sitting, and lying down on their sides, and think deeply about the creation of the heavens and the earth, (saying): "Our Lord! You have not created (all) this without purpose, glory to You! (Exalted be You above all that they associate with You as partners). Give us salvation from the torment of the Fire." - Qur'ān, 3:190-191

---

[16]https://Islāmqa.info/en/answers/103390/

Islām emphasizes the importance of regularly engaging with nature as a form of mindfulness. It boldly asserts that it is the natural religion for which humanity was created, helping to explain the profound peace of mind it offers.

"So set your face (O Muhammad) towards the religion of pure Islāmic Monotheism Hanīfā (worship none but Allāh Alone) Allāh's Fitrah (i.e. Allāh's Islāmic Monotheism), with which He has created mankind. No change let there be in Khalq–illāh (i.e. the Religion of Allāh Islāmic Monotheism), that is the straight religion, but most of men know not." - Qur'ān, 30:30

05

Patience and Gratitude: In Hardship and Ease

L IFE presents us with both periods of hardship and ease. As discussed in previous chapters, both can serve as sources of good or evil, depending on our willingness to accept and manage them. The most reliable way to ensure that both positive and negative situations work in our favor is to remain steadfast on the straight path—staying true to what we know and believing in the Creed of Islām.

Sticking to the straight path must not depend on the good or the bad that befalls us, we must muster on the path, regardless. The whole idea of someone moving straight is that he does not go to the right or left. Zigzagging means we are not truly moving straight, even if we are making small progress. Being straight means remaining determined and ignoring temptations to veer right or left, regardless of incentives or obstacles. The apparent ease on your right may entice you, while the hardships on your left may distract you. Nevertheless, you must remain committed to your faith and follow the straight path.

Regardless of Hardship

Your steadfastness on the straight path, even in extreme difficulty, will lead to success.

"O you who have believed, be patient, and endure, and remain stationed, and be mindful of Allāh that you may succeed."[1] — Qur'ān, 3:200

Mindfulness, which we have discussed several times, is crucial for achieving clarity and remaining focused on the straight path. Here, Allāh encourages believers to endure hardship with patience. He calls us to stand firm, like steadfast sentinels protecting a community during times of war. Picture guarding your faith with the same vigilance as defending a fortress against an impending threat. Stay alert, much like a sentinel overseeing an armory during battle.

In this context, you are urged to safeguard your commitment to the straight path, recognizing that it comes with its own challenges and tribulations. Even in the direst circumstances, such as war, we are encouraged not to abandon our faith. Consider the struggles we face that may not be life-threatening; a true believer must persevere and adhere to the principles of his creed. Difficult

---

[1]This specific translation is from Ṣaḥīḥ International

times should never be a reason to abandon faith or drive us away from the straight path. Remember, challenges do not last forever, and with unwavering faith, we are more than capable of navigating through them.

The Principles of Hardship

Every hardship you encounter should evoke three key responses in your mind.

- **First**, remember that you will never be burdened with more than you can bear.

- **Second**, understand that after every hardship, there comes ease.

- **Third**, know that you will be rewarded for every hardship endured, often more so than for moments of ease.

Regarding the first principle, Allāh says,

"Allāh burdens not a person beyond his scope..." - Qur'ān, 2:286

This verse emphasizes that every Islāmic ruling is within your ability to uphold. There may be times when you feel that breaking these rules is the only way out, but this mindset contradicts the message of the verse.

For example, a student might feel so desperate to pass an exam that they consider cheating due to their lack of preparation. However, a true believer understands there is always a way to avoid sin, even if it means sacrificing a short-term gain.

Similarly, someone might enter a business believing that success can only come through dishonest means, thinking, *"Everyone does it."* Yet a believer chooses to respect the limits set by Allāh, knowing that these boundaries are not burdensome, even if they seem so to others due to a lack of understanding.

Take a person who wishes to study at an Islāmic university with age restrictions. While they want to do good, they may not meet the admission criteria because of their age. A steadfast individual recognizes that lying to get around this rule is unacceptable and remains truthful, even if it costs them admission and acceptance into the University. This is because he knows Allāh ,says,

"...And whoever transgresses the limits ordained by Allāh, then such are the Zalimūn (wrong-doers, etc.)..." - Qur'ān, 2:229

The core belief here is that you have the innate ability to follow all rules, as they are not intended to overwhelm you.

There are instances where exceptions to these rules apply, particularly in cases of necessity. For example, if adhering to a rule threatens a believer's safety or well-being, they may be permitted to take the forbidden option. This allowance exists to protect human life. Ibn Nujaym's *Al-Ashyā' wan-Nazā'ir* lists three such exceptions:

- **First** is eating carrion or forbidden meat, like pork, when facing starvation.

- **Second**, renouncing faith verbally under extreme duress or torture.

- **Lastly**, dying as a martyr while defending oneself against an aggressor.

The second principle regarding hardship is that ease is always near no matter how severe the difficulties may seem, especially for those who remain patient and do good. Such individuals will be rewarded for their perseverance, and their status will be elevated before Allāh.

"So, surely with hardship comes ease. Surely with hardship comes ease."[2] - Qur'ān, 94:5

We can be assured that ease is near whenever we encounter calamity or a setback. Allāh emphasizes this twice, and linguistically, this does not just mean two hardships; it implies multiple forms of ease. Thus, we can conclude that ease is greater than the hardship.

The Prophet (PBUH) said,

"A hardship cannot outweigh two eases," indicating that hardship cannot overcome both times of ease that are promised to the believers, the ease in this world, nor the ease that is promised to them in the next world.[3]

If the hardships of this world seem overwhelming, they will never overshadow the ease that awaits in the afterlife. The believer will be richly rewarded for every hardship faced during their time on Earth.

---

[2]Translation in this instance is Dr. Mustafā Khattāb, The Clear Qur'ān

[3]Tafsīr al-Tabarī on Surah Ash-Sharḥ 94:6

The third important principle regarding hardship is that a believer is rightfully compensated for enduring it. The Prophet Muhammad (PBUH) said:

"No fatigue, nor disease, nor sorrow, nor sadness, nor hurt, nor distress befalls a Muslim, even if it were the prick he receives from a thorn, but that Allāh expiates some of his sins for that."[4]

He (PBUH) also said,

"How wonderful is the affair of the believer, for his affairs are all good, and this applies to no one but the believer. If something good happens to him, he is grateful to Allāh, and that is good for him. If something harmful happens to him, he is patient, and that is good for him."[5]

Regardless of Ease

Surviving hardship and achieving ease in this world—whether through finding effective solutions or gaining peace of mind from understanding the principles of hardship—is just the beginning. Equally important is handling that peace and feeling of relief after hardship passes and peace finally arrives, calming the storms of struggle.

Consider a man who faced poverty and, after much hard work and prayer, was blessed with wealth. Instead of remaining grateful, he becomes complacent in his worship, celebrating his "success" by indulging in forbidden pleasures such as alcohol.

---

[4] Ṣaḥīḥ al-Bukhārī, Hadīth No. 5641 and Ṣaḥīḥ Muslim, Hadīth No. 2573

[5] Ṣaḥīḥ Muslim, Hadīth No. 2999

Similarly, think of a woman who prayed for a child and, after enduring the challenges of pregnancy, receives that blessing. Instead of expressing gratitude through worship, she throws lavish parties, indulging in practices that disobey Allāh, and ignoring the significance of her blessings.

This misuse of ease can be seen in various aspects of life—marriages, promotions, or increased status. Even within religious circles, some who complete the memorization or recitation of the Qur'ān often celebrate in ways that displease Allāh.

We also see the rich, saved from poverty, using their wealth for illicit relationships, forgetting that true ease requires not just effort in this world but also preparation for the hereafter. Allāh reminds us,

> *"O you who have attained faith, be mindful of Allāh, and let every soul look what it has put forth for tomorrow, and be mindful of Allāh; indeed, Allāh is All-Aware of what you do."*[6]
> – Qur'an, 59:18

Once again, the theme of mindfulness emerges, as highlighted in the previous verse. Here, Allāh encourages everyone to work diligently to ensure their good deeds are recorded for eternity so they weigh heavily on their scales on the Day of Accountability. A believer who neglects to seek Allāh's mercy and paradise may not fully grasp this message.

Ease should inspire us to do better, not serve as a license for disobedience. Just as one might stray from the

---

[6]Translation in this instance is from Dr. Muhammad Asad's translation, The Message of the Qur'ān.

path by cutting corners during hardship, the one who disobeys in times of ease also veers off the straight path.

Incidentally, ease can be as much a trial as hardship. Staying true to the straight path means ensuring that neither difficulty nor comfort leads us away from our obligations in Islām. The Prophet (PBUH) expressed his concerns about the potential pitfalls during times of ease when he said,

"By Allāh, it is not poverty I fear for you; rather, I fear you will be given the wealth of the world, just as it was given to those before you. You will compete for it just as they competed for it and it will ruin you just as it ruined them."[7]

We see that the Prophet (PBUH) was more concerned about our actions during times of ease than hardships.

So, what principles can we adopt to navigate these moments of comfort?

Principles of Ease

During times of ease, it is important to embrace certain principles to help maintain your commitment to the straight path. These principles are Acceptance, Gratitude, Humility, and Facilitation.

1. Acceptance

The first step when ease arrives, or even just before it, is to recognize it as a gift from Allāh. Understand that He does not intend hardship for us, especially in matters

---

[7] Ṣaḥīḥ al-Bukhārī, Ḥadīth No. 6425

of faith. As Allāh noted when discussing those for whom fasting during Ramadan is prescribed,

"...Allāh intends for you ease, and He does not want to make things difficult for you. (He wants that you) must complete the same number (of days), and that you must magnify Allāh for having guided you so that you may be grateful to Him." -
Qur'ān, 2:185

A fundamental principle is that Allāh desires **ease** for us, **not hardship**. The Prophet Muhammad (PBUH) emphasized this message about ease:

"Religion is easy, and no one overburdens himself in his religion, but he will be unable to continue in that way. So do not be extremists but try to be near perfection and receive the good tidings that you will be rewarded."[8]

If the general principle for religious worship is to embrace ease, this applies even more to our everyday lives. When a religious command comes with a degree of ease, we should not, out of zeal, complicate it. Instead, we should focus on being consistent in our practices. Similarly, when worldly matters come easily, we should not over-complicate them. We are encouraged to enjoy these blessings of ease and express our gratitude to our Lord and Creator.

---

[8] Ṣaḥīḥ al-Bukhārī, Hadīth No. 39

2. Gratitude

Gratitude involves offering praise and thanks to Allāh while engaging in acts of worship that reflect our appreciation for His countless blessings. It begins with recognizing what may seem inconsequential. This is also applicable to our relationships with others. The Prophet Muhammad (PBUH) said:

"Whoever is not grateful for a little will not be grateful for a lot."[9]

This is crucial because we often postpone our gratitude until we experience significant ease or major achievements. The Prophet (PBUH) reminds us that if we fail to express thanks for the small blessings, we may become ungrateful for the larger ones.

"And (remember) when your Lord proclaimed: "If you give thanks (by accepting Faith and worshipping none but Allāh), I will give you more (of My Blessings), but if you are thankless (i.e. disbelievers), verily! My Punishment is indeed severe."" - Qur'ān, 14:7

We should never overlook what may seem small; it is essential to recognize and appreciate even the little blessings. By doing so, we open ourselves to receiving greater favors from Allāh. This is a vital practice that every believer should prioritize.

As regards showing gratitude to others, the Prophet Muhammad (PBUH) said:

---

[9] Sunan Abī Dāwūd, Hadīth No. 4817 and Sunan Ibn Mājah, Hadīth No. 3826

"He who is ungrateful to the people is ungrateful to Allah."[10]

3. Humility

After accepting ease and expressing gratitude, we must approach life with humility. Humility encompasses several aspects. First, we must acknowledge that everything we possess is a gift from Allāh, far beyond our efforts or intelligence. Second, we must instinctively remember that when hardship comes our way, it is to Allāh that we should turn for support.

"And whatever of blessings and good things you have, it is from Allāh. Then, when harm touches you, unto Him you cry aloud for help." - Qur'ān, 16:53

Thirdly, those who are favored must consistently remember that humility is a pathway to elevation, as the Messenger of Allāh said:

"Charity does not decrease wealth, no one forgives another except that Allāh increases his honor, and no one humbles himself for the sake of Allāh except that Allāh raises his status."[11]

With this understanding, the final principle becomes much easier to embrace.

---

[10]Sunan Abī Dāwūd, Hadīth No. 4811
[11]Ṣaḥīḥ Muslim, Hadīth No. 2588

4. Facilitation

Those who experience ease have a communal responsibility to help others find their own ease. This can manifest through acts of generosity, being accommodating in dealings with others, showing patience with those facing challenges, and providing sound advice. Allāh speaks about charity, saying:

"Let the rich man spend according to his means, and the man whose resources are restricted, let him spend according to what Allāh has given him. Allāh puts no burden on any person beyond what He has given him. Allāh will grant after hardship, ease." – Qur'an, 65:7

The Prophet Muhammad (PBUH) said:

"Make things easy for people and do not make them difficult. Give them good tidings and do not make them turn away."[12]

The Hadīth above highlights two or three principles related to bringing ease to others. It encourages us to make things easier for people, to share good news, and not to turn anyone away. Additionally, he (PBUH) stated that:

"The believer who mixes with people and is patient with their harm has a greater reward than the believer who does not mix with people, nor is patient with their harm."[13]

---

[12] Ṣaḥīḥ Muslim, Hadīth No. 1734
[13] Sunan Ibn Mājah, Hadīth No. 4032

Engaging with people, supporting them, and positively influencing their lives is commendable. Regarding those who are owed debt, he (PBUH) said:

"A man among those before you was called to account in the Hereafter. Nothing good was found with him but that he was lenient in his dealings with people, and he would order his servant to relieve the debts of those in hardship. Allāh Almighty said: We are more worthy of such actions, so overlook his sins."[14]

The key is to offer help, just as Allāh has helped us. We'll conclude this chapter with a story shared by the Prophet (PBUH):

"Verily, there were three among the children of Israel whom Allāh Almighty intended to test: a leper, a bald man, and a blind man. He sent an angel to them and he came to the leper, saying: What would you love most? The leper said: I want a beautiful color and beautiful skin, for people have shunned me. The angel wiped over him and it had gone away, then he was given a beautiful color and beautiful skin. The angel said: Which property would you love most? The man said: Camels. Thus, he was given a pregnant camel. The angel said: May Allāh bless you in it. The angel came to the bald man, saying: What would you love most? The bald man said: Beautiful hair and to be rid of this, for people have shunned me. The angel wiped over him and it had gone away, then he was given beautiful hair. The angel said: Which property would you love most? The man said: Cows. Thus, he was given a pregnant cow. The angel said: May Allāh bless you in it. The angel came to the blind man, saying: What would you love most?

---

[14]Sunan al-Tirmidhī, Hadīth No. 1307

The blind man said: For Allāh to return my sight so I can see people. The angel wiped over him, then Allāh returned his sight. The angel said: Which property would you love most? The man said: Sheep. Thus, he was given a pregnant sheep. The animals had grown and given birth such that one man had a valley of camels, another had a valley of cows, and another had a valley of sheep. Then, the angel came to the former leper while disguised in the shape and appearance of a leper, saying: I am a poor man, bereft of my livelihood while on a journey, none can take care of my needs today but Allāh and then you, so I ask by the One who gave you beautiful color and beautiful skin and a wealth of camels to help me reach my destination! The man said: I have many duties. The angel said to him: It is as if I recognize you, were you not a leper shunned by people, in poverty, but Allāh gave this to you? The man said: I have inherited it from my forefathers. The angel said: If you are lying, then may Allāh return you to what you were before! The angel came to the former bald man in a similar appearance, saying the same as he had said to the leper and the man responded the same way. The angel said: If you are lying, then may Allāh return you to what you were before! The angel came to the blind man in a similar form, saying: I am a poor man and wayfarer, bereft of my livelihood while on a journey, none can take care of my needs today but Allāh and then you, so I ask by the One who returned your sight and gave you sheep to help me reach my destination! The man said: I was once a blind man and Allāh returned my sight, I was poor and He enriched me, so take whatever you wish for, by Allāh, I will not dispute you today in whatever you take for Allāh's sake. The angel said: Keep your property, for I was only sent to test you and Allāh is pleased with you but angry with your two companions."[15]

---

[15] Ṣaḥīḥ al-Bukhārī, Ḥadīth No. 3464, Ṣaḥīḥ Muslim, Ḥadīth No.

Whether in ease or hardship, this blessing of gratitude is bestowed upon only a select few among humanity.

"They worked for him what he desired, (making) high rooms, images, basins as large as reservoirs, and (cooking) cauldrons fixed (in their places). "Work you, O family of Dāwūd (David), with thanks!" But few of My slaves are grateful." - Qur'ān, 34:13

2964

06

A Foundation of Clarity –
The Principle of Tawhīd

I^T is often said that your beliefs are wrong when viewed through the lens of some other religion. This assertion assumes that the existence of many divergent religions with different doctrines will either mean whatever religion one follows is fine, or all religions are wrong. Such reasoning, unfortunately, lacks a connection to reality. That everyone claims to own the car does not mean it has no owner. It also does not mean everyone owns it either. A true seeker of truth must consider several possibilities.

The proliferation of religions can often be traced back to a lack of clarity among the laity and the clergy regarding the core tenets of faith as it relates to the concept of God. In contrast, Islām does not suffer this problem, unburdened by these ambiguities.

The Islāmic principle of faith is clear, with the under-lying foundational principle being rooted in belief in the Oneness of Allāh (Tawhīd). This means acknowledging that only Allāh is the True Lord, deserving of all worship, and embracing His names and attributes as He has described Himself in the Qur'ān.

"Say (O Muhammad): "He is Allāh, (the) One.
Allāh-us-Samad (The Self-Sufficient Master, Whom all
creatures need, He neither eats nor drinks). He begets not, nor
was He begotten; And there is none co-equal or comparable
unto Him." - Qur'ān, 112:1-4

"And your Ilāh (God) is One Ilāh (God – Allāh), Lā ilāha illā
Huwa (there is none who has the right to be worshiped but He),
the Most Beneficent, the Most Merciful." - Qur'ān, 2:163

Allāh describes Himself as eternally One, Unique, Self-Sufficient, Most Gracious, and Most Merciful. This verse clearly articulates the uniqueness of Allāh's Lordship while simultaneously spotlighting some of His attributes. Through-out the Qur'ān, you will find references to many of His glorious names and attributes.

The guidance provided by these verses helps Muslims attain clarity about the essence of God, firmly rejecting any doctrine that suggests God exists as part of a pantheon of deities, whether they be objects or beings. Even regarding certain qualities we share as humans with Him to some degree, we reject that anyone possesses them in the same way as God or vice versa.

While such ideas may seem far-fetched, history has seen individuals claim divinity or assert they have the power to forgive sins and the list goes on. For a Muslim who understands these verses, recognizing the fallacy of such claims becomes evident. They can discern the truth, knowing, for instance, that God Almighty is not part of a trinity, as the Qur'ān clearly states;

"Surely, disbelievers are those who said: "Allāh is the third of the three (in a Trinity)." But there is no ilāh (god) (none who has the right to be worshiped) but One Ilāh (God -Allāh). And if they cease not from what they say, verily, a painful torment will befall the disbelievers among them." – Qur'ān, 5:73

If the concept of God was ambiguous, how could the average person in the laity follow? Evidently, the world is not filled with *brainiacs*; most people possess average intellect. A merciful God would ensure that the essentials of His message are clear so that no one—whether a king or a commoner, a prince or a pauper—faces confusion. Often, what we perceive as vague is, in fact, quite clear. One good example is the question of what constitutes the right religion and who God truly is. This stands out as particularly straightforward, with very few and hardly substantial counterclaims.

In the Qur'ān, Allāh clearly defines Who He is and describes His attributes without ambiguity. This clarity is a claim that no other religious text boldly asserts.

To illustrate, consider the ownership of a property: if I present a legitimate receipt and you present another, confusion may arise. We might argue, bicker, and even take our dispute to court to determine which receipt is valid.

However, if I produce an authentic receipt containing all relevant details—such as the property's description, my name, the purchase cost, date, and place—while your receipt lacks these specifics, the case will clearly favor me. All they need is to verify the information I provided.

A lot of wild claims have been made to call Jesus God. Had he been God, aside from the fact that it directly contradicts everything we know about God's immortality, among other things, he would have declared it himself unequivocally, as lucid as can be read in the Quranic verses above. Not a single claim came from him.

Understanding the Names and Attributes of Allāh and choosing to worship Him alone as our Lord helps reduce confusion, especially when discerning the true message from God. This can be likened to a student attending a school far from his guardian. While his fellow students may know little about their own parents, he deeply understands his. If letters from their parents were mixed up, identifying his letter would be like finding needles in a haystack.

However, the student who knows his guardian well would have an easier time sorting through the letters. For instance, if he finds a letter that says, *"Your mother and I will always love you,"* he would recognize immediately that it is not his since his father passed away when he was very young. A letter saying, *"In all my travels, I have never seen a child as well-mannered as you,"* would also be easy for him to dismiss, knowing his mother rarely travels due to her demanding job.

Ultimately, he would identify a letter with contents only his widowed mother could express, leading him home.

In contrast, other students, unsure of their parents, might be easily swayed by any letter, leading to increased confusion.

The more we understand the Names and Attributes of God Almighty, the easier it becomes to recognize what aligns with His Divine Essence. Only Islām meticulously addresses this, and when you immerse yourself in these meanings, they become evident in your daily life. Tawhīd is the belief that Allāh is One, with no partners or associates in His Lordship *(Rubūbiyyah)*, His Divinity *(Ulūhiyyah)*, or His Names and Attributes *(Al-asmā Wa al-Sifāt)*.

Tawhīd al-Rubūbiyyah – Oneness of Lordship

This means believing that Allāh is One and Unique in His acts of creation, Sovereignty, Control, the granting of life and death, and a string of others.

"...Surely, His is the Creation and Commandment. Blessed be Allāh, the Lord of the 'Ālamīn (mankind, jinns and all that exists)!" - Qur'ān, 7:54

These verses may seem familiar or even cliché, but it is important to recognize that other religions do not make such bold claims. For instance, someone might assert, "Jesus is God," but if you were to ask, *"Did Jesus create the world and everything in it, including you?"* they might hesitate. This hesitation reflects an instinctive awareness of truth that challenges their initial belief. Allāh alludes to this when He speaks of the disbelievers of old:

"And if you ask them who created them, they will surely say: "Allāh". How then are they turned away (from the worship of

Allāh, Who created them)?" - Qur'ān, 43:87

Once more, Allāh draws our attention to this contradiction:

"If you were to ask them: "Who has created the heavens and the earth and subjected the sun and the moon?" They will surely reply: "Allāh." How then are they deviating (as polytheists and disbelievers)?" - Qur'ān, 29:61

It is challenging enough to claim that a man is God; it is even more absurd to suggest that he created you, the stars, the sun, the moon, and the sky that he is walking under himself as a man. Allāh further emphasizes this by saying:

"If you were to ask them: "Who sends down water (rain) from the sky, and gives life therewith to the earth after its death?" They will surely reply: "Allāh." Say: "All the praises and thanks be to Allāh!" Nay! Most of them have no sense." - Qur'ān, 29:63

The disbelievers of the past, and some even today, acknowledge that Allāh, in His solitude, created the universe and all within it and that He reigns supreme over the affairs of the world. Yet, tragically, they persist in denial that He alone deserves absolute obedience and worship.

In contemporary society, we encounter individuals who may accept Allāh as the Creator of all things but behave in ways that contradict the fundamental belief that He is the Sovereign and Controller of all affairs.

This belief is contradicted when people attribute predestination to forces other than Allāh, implying that events occur outside His control. Phrases like *"untimely death"* often arise, suggesting that when someone dies in their prime, it was not meant to be, and thus God did not intend for that *"untimely death."* Consequently, some may believe that such a death is caused by other superstitious spiritual forces, which they mistakenly think have the power to take or grant life.

Others may believe they can attain great wealth by circumventing Allāh's decree, turning to unholy sources for what is ultimately reserved for the Controller of the seen and unseen universe.

Like their predecessors, some individuals accept parts of Allāh's sovereignty (Rubūbiyyah) yet still choose to worship others alongside Him, thereby undermining the second aspect of Tawhīd.

Tawhīd al-Ulūhiyyah – Worshipping Allāh Alone

One unique aspect of Islām is that its Prophets never asked to be worshiped. In fact, it is a grave sin to worship a prophet of Allāh or attribute divine qualities to them.

In contrast, some religions have founders who seek undeserved reverence, either by claiming to be God or suggesting they have God-like qualities. According to Tawhīd, certain attributes belong solely to Allāh, and neither we nor the Prophets, Muhammad (PEUH) being the last of them, share these.

Even great figures who never claimed to be above ordinary humans are worshiped in some religions after their death. In others, religious leaders subtly seek worship, encouraging prayers directed to God through them, mentioning their names in prayers, or seeking certain acts of 'righteousness' for their personal aggrandizement rather than for God Almighty.

Tawhīd al-Ulūhiyyah emphasizes that all internal and external worship should be directed solely to Allāh, without worshiping anyone or anything else, regardless of their status. Allāh emphasizes this in His teachings.

"And your Lord has decreed that you worship none but Him..." - Qur'ān, 17:23

"Worship Allāh and join none with Him in worship..."... - Qur'ān, 4:36

This establishes God Almighty as the highest authority, reserving true worship exclusively for Him. Anyone seeking worship for themselves or worshiping anything other than Allāh is straying from the right path.

This is the hallmark of sincerity. It makes pleasing Allāh the ultimate goal of all our actions, with pleasing others taking a distant third place. We should only seek to please people if it does not provoke Allāh's disapproval, reflecting a clear commitment to the right way.

To truly understand the devotion of worshiping Allāh alone, we must grasp what worship means. This aspect of Tawhīd is known as Tawhīd al-Ulūhiyyah, which signifies complete devotion to Allāh with love and reverence. We must never turn our devotion to anyone else or love anyone more than Allāh. Our love for Allāh is demonstrated through our unwavering obedience to His commands, as highlighted by the teachings of Islām.

"Say, O Prophet, 'If you sincerely love Allāh, then follow me;
Allāh will love you and forgive your sins. For Allāh is
All-Forgiving, Most Merciful.'" - Qur'ān, 3:31

The noble Prophet Muhammad (PBUH) was reported to have said:

"There is no obedience to anyone if it is disobedience to Allāh.
Verily, obedience is only in good conduct."[1]

We might think that the person we obey in disobedience of Allāh would outright say, "Disobey Allāh!" However, often, they are subtle in their influence. They may encourage disobedience, and we comply, even as Allāh calls us to do the opposite.

Tawhīd al-Ulūhiyyah, or *Tawhīd al-'Ibādah* (oneness in worship), emphasizes that our worship of Allāh is reflected in our obedience to His commands. This brings us back to the theme of obedience, which is rooted in love for Allāh.

This concept is also known as *Tawhīd al-Talab wa'l-Qasd wa'l-Irādah* (Oneness of goal, purpose, and intention), meaning we seek nothing but the pleasure of Allāh, worshiping Him sincerely.

This is why ostentation, or showing off, is forbidden in Islām. The term *Al-Riyaa* refers to performing acts of worship merely to be seen by others, aiming to gain praise and admiration from people. Allāh warns against this, saying,

"So woe unto those performers of Salāt (prayers) (hypocrites),
Who delay their Salāt (prayer) from their stated fixed times,

---

[1]Ṣaḥīḥ al-Bukhārī, Hadīth No. 7257, Ṣaḥīḥ Muslim, Hadīth No. 1840

those who do good deeds only to be seen (of men)..." - Qur'ān,
107:4-6

The Messenger of Allāh, Muhammad (PBUH) said:

*"The thing I fear most for you is the minor shirk: al-Riyā. Allāh
will say on the Day of Resurrection when He is recompensing
people for their deeds: 'Go to those for whom you were showing off
in the world and see if you can find any reward with them.'"*[2]

Tawhīd al-Asmā was-Sifāt: Affirming Allah's Names and Attributes

The final aspect of Tawhīd relates to the Names and
Attributes of God Almighty. When we truly affirm these
names, it becomes easier to reconnect with Him and recognize and reject those who falsely claim divine status.
Understanding God's attributes helps us appreciate His
daily blessings and navigate challenging questions others
may struggle to answer.

History is filled with individuals who have claimed
divine powers, asserting they are God or part of a divine
realm. While we often focus on the delusions of their followers, we may overlook that these claimants are often
just as misguided and intoxicated by their own lies. Such
confusion stems from a misunderstanding of the concept
of God and a lack of knowledge about God's true names
and attributes.

For instance, someone who understands Allāh as *Al-
Alīm* (All-Knowing) can see through the façade of these

---

[2]Musnad Imām Ahmad, Hadīth No. 23636

claimants, recognizing that a fellow human who lacks self-awareness cannot possibly claim divinity.

Knowing Allāh as the One Who gives and takes life brings comfort when facing the death of a loved one. This understanding does not prevent us from feeling the pain of losing a loved one or seeking justice in cases of homicide, but it reassures us that every soul must experience death as decreed by Allāh, who, in turn, rewards our patience.

Similarly, recognizing Allāh as *Al-Fattāh* (the Opener) helps us appreciate unexpected solutions to problems. This attribute connects Allāh to countless mercies and provisions that we may receive in this life and the next. We no longer deceive ourselves into thinking success is solely linked to our efforts; even hard work is ultimately a favor from Allāh.

Furthermore, understanding Allāh's attributes allows us to quickly address existential questions that may trouble those following unclear creeds. For example, many grapple with the concept of evil, questioning whether God permits it and, if so, why. Some misguided individuals attribute evil to the Devil, but when asked how the Devil can seemingly do more harm than God can do good, they are left speechless.

This confusion has driven many to atheism, yet they could find clarity in Islām's teachings. The believer knows from Allāh's names that He can withhold or bestow wealth, give life or cause death, punish or forgive, and so forth.

Tawhīd al-Asmā was-Sifāt has two key components: first, affirming all of God's Names as mentioned in the Qur'ān or by His Prophet; second, denying any notion that Allāh could be fallible or comparable to His creation.

"...There is nothing like unto Him, and He is the All-Hearer, the All-Seer." - Qur'ān, 42:11

Part of this involves avoiding descriptions of Allāh that do not reflect His Majesty. We should describe Him only as He describes Himself or as His Messenger has conveyed. Even when Allāh uses attributes that can apply to humans, we recognize that both are incomparable, for nothing resembles Him.

For example, We do not consider ourselves children of God; we are merely His creations and servants (the term slave is often used in translations for this same context). We do not attribute any biological characteristics to Allāh, as He has never done so Himself. Therefore, there is no special Son of God; He has no sons or children, period. Consequently, we do not refer to God as "Father." He is our Creator and Sustainer, and human attributes are far removed from His nature.

"And there is none like unto Him." - Qur'ān, 112:4

"And (both) the Jews and the Christians say: "We are the children of Allāh and His loved ones." Say: "Why then does He punish you for your sins?" Nay, you are but human beings; of those He has created, He forgives whom He wills, and He punishes whom He wills. And to Allāh belongs the dominion of the heavens and the earth and all that is between them, and to Him is the return (of all)." - Qur'ān 5:18

This is one out of six Articles of the Islāmic faith, and Al-Qurtubī (may Allāh have mercy on him) said: "This is the prescribed belief referred to in the Hadīth of Jibrīl (peace be upon him), in which he said to the Prophet (peace and blessings of Allāh be upon him):

Tell me about faith (Īmān). He said: "It is to believe in Allāh, His angels, His Books, His Messengers, and the Last Day, and to believe in the divine decree, both good and bad." He said: You have spoken the truth."[3]

---

[3]Tafsīr Al-Qurtubī 1/252, Musnad Imām Ahmad, Hadīth No. 191

07

Of Justice and Obedience –
Belief in the Angels

P ART of what humbles a person in the worship of Allāh is the knowledge of the existence of other creatures, especially in the case of the Angels, ever-obedient creatures, unwavering in their loyalty to Allāh. For example, If a person were to become arrogant in the process of worship, then reflecting on the vastness and incredible abilities of the angels as regards their worship can serve as a powerful reminder, swiftly bringing them to their knees in humility.

It is narrated by Abdullāh ibn Mas'ūd (R.A) that,

"The Prophet (PBUH) saw Angel Jibrīl in his true form, and he had six hundred wings, each of which filled the horizon. From his wings, there were multi-colored drops of pearls and coral

falling."[1]

And the Prophet (PBUH) said about the size of a particular angel,

"I have been permitted to speak of one of the angels of Allāh who is one of the bearers of the Throne. The distance between his earlobe and his shoulder is a journey of seven hundred years."[2]

If these heavenly beings—remarkable in their abilities and grandeur—can worship Allāh tirelessly, then even the mightiest human should find humility. He should recognize that his devotion serves his own benefit, as Allāh is already worshiped by countless creatures. The angels, in their multitude, are lovingly described in the Prophet's teachings about the places they frequent for worship:

"Then the Much-Frequented House was raised up for me, and I asked Jibrīl (about it). He said: 'This is the Much-Frequented House. Every day seventy thousand angels enter it and when they depart from it, they never return to it.'"[3]

A believer on the straight path finds humility and strives to worship diligently. If you choose to honor someone who is honored by no one else and is rarely recognized, it might be a trivial encounter, and you would likely not pay much careful attention to how you go about it. This is especially so because Whatever you offer to them as an honor has no benchmark for its comparison or appraisal; the fellow was

---

[1] Ṣaḥīḥ Muslim, Ḥadīth No. 174c
[2] Sunan Abī Dāwūd, Ḥadīth No. 4727
[3] Ṣaḥīḥ al-Bukhārī, Ḥadīth No. 3207

not receiving anything close to it. However, if you were to host a revered king with a vast following, you would make every effort to meet or even exceed the expected standards.

In this light, Allāh's mercy on fallible humans is evident. Unlike the Angels, who are never disobedient, He has not set the bar for us as high as He did for them; instead, He encourages us to repent from our sins when we err and strive for improvement. This understanding shows the wisdom in our belief in angels, which is a fundamental part of the six Articles of Faith in Islām.

Angels belong to the Unseen, and our belief in them deepens our faith in Allāh. If religion was based solely on miracles and clear signs, it would not require genuine belief, as there would be no space for trust and faith in the Unseen. Our belief in the Unseen, as commanded by Allāh, is a testament to our faith.

"...This is the Book (the Qur'ān), whereof there is no doubt, a guidance to those who are Al-Muttūn [the pious and righteous...]. Who believe in the Ghaib (the unseen) and perform As-Salāt (Iqamat-as-Salāt), and spend out of what we have provided for them" - Qur'ān, 2:2-3

Our belief in the Unseen is a profound testament to our trust in Allāh's perfect knowledge, acknowledging that some matters lie beyond our limited understanding. We recognize Allāh's Mercy and Grace in believing in angels, particularly in the advantage fallible, righteous humans possess above these celestial angels. This is in specific regard to the fact that we get both free will and an opportunity to seek forgiveness and be forgiven after we have erred. This reflects His boundless mercy and forgiveness. As the Prophet of Allāh (PBUH) said,

"Verily, I see what you do not see, and I hear what you do not hear. The heaven is creaking, and it should creak, for there is no space in it the width of four fingers, but there is an angel there, placing his forehead in prostration to Allāh."[4]

Human worship of Allāh, while significant in frequency, is dwarfed by that of the angels. Yet Allāh's mercy toward us is unwavering, sometimes elevating the righteous but fallible among us above even the never-disobedient angels. This reflects His grace in recognizing our inherent struggle against evil. If we patiently resist our desires and strive for goodness, our human challenges and inclination towards evil can become a source of abundant reward. In Islām, the theme of forgiveness is profoundly emphasized beyond human imagination.

In the Hadīth of Abū Huraira, Allāh's Messenger (may peace and blessings of Allāh be upon him) reportedly said:

"By Him in Whose Hand is my life, if you were not to commit sin, Allāh would sweep you out of existence and He would replace (you by) those people who would commit sin and seek forgiveness from Allāh, and He would have pardoned them."[5]

Allāh detests sin, yet when we stumble, His love for forgiveness shines through. This is beautifully reflected in the well-known prayers,

---

[4]Sunan al-Tirmidhī, Hadīth No. 2312, Musnad Imām Ahmad, Hadīth No. 20452

[5]Ṣaḥīḥ Muslim, Hadīth No. 2749

"O Allāh, You are Forgiving and love forgiveness, so forgive me"[6]

This should serve as a benchmark for parents raising children. If God can be quick to forgive grown adults, we must learn to love our children and tolerate their mistakes as we gradually teach and guide them through life.

The diversity in Allāh's creatures, especially in the case of angels sheds some light on Allāh's promise to purify all inhabitants of paradise, ensuring they will never sin again. It provides confidence for a believer in Allah's promise of their transformation into elegant beings in Jannah (paradise).In paradise, worship will revolve solely around the remembrance of Allāh without any more work or effort needed. As the Prophet (PBUH) said,

"The people of Paradise will eat and drink therein, but they will not blow their noses or defecate or urinate. Their food there will turn into burps and sweat like musk. They will be caused to recite Tasbīh (glorification) and praise, as they are caused to breathe."[7]

Another significant benefit of believing in angels is the establishment of justice. Allāh is never unjust, and even though there is no one to challenge Him, He has forbidden injustice for Himself.

The Messenger of Allāh, peace and blessings of Allāh be upon him, said,

"Allāh Almighty said: O My servants, I have forbidden injustice for Myself and I have forbidden it among you, so do not oppress one another..."[8]

---

[6]Sunan al-Tirmidhī, Hadīth No. 3513
[7]Ṣaḥīḥ Muslim, Hadīth No. 2835c
[8]Ṣaḥīḥ Muslim, Hadīth No 2577a

This is the paramount importance of justice in Islām, as the belief in angels demonstrates its significance. Part of the functions of Angels is to witness our actions, recording both our good deeds and our missteps, the latter with greater restraint. Although Allāh, the All-Knowing, does not need these records to know what you did or did not do, He created certain angels to document our actions as additional ample evidence, thus establishing justice. Allāh says about the angels and their record-keeping,

"(Remember!) that the two receivers (recording angels) receive (each human being after he or she has attained the age of puberty), one sitting on the right and one on the left (to note his or her actions). Man does not utter any word except that with him is an observer prepared [to record]." - Qur'ān, 50:17-18

"But verily, over you (are appointed angels in charge of mankind) to watch you, Kirāman (honorable) Kātibīn writing down (your deeds), they know all that you do. - Qur'ān, 82:10-12

As mentioned earlier, these records are taken in a way that tends to favor recording your good deeds more than your evil, a display of Allāh's Mercy. The Messenger of Allāh (PBUH) said:

"The angel of the left raises his pen (to write the sin) for six hours (so that the sinner might repent) before he writes it."[9]

In another narration, he (PBUH) said:

---

[9] Al-Mu'jam al-Kabīr, Hadīth No. 7765, declared Hassan by Albāni in Ṣaḥīḥ al-Jami', 2097

"Whosoever intended to perform a good deed, but did not do it, then Allāh writes it down with Himself as a complete good deed. And if he intended to perform it and then did perform it, then Allāh writes it down with Himself as from ten good deeds up to seven hundred times, up to many times multiplied. And if he intended to perform an evil deed, but did not do it, then Allāh writes it down with Himself as a complete good deed. And if he intended it [i.e., the evil deed] and then performed it, then Allāh writes it down as one evil deed."[10]

In summary, the major idea about angels keeping records, despite Allāh's complete knowledge of all that exists, is the establishment of justice.

"And with Him are the keys of the Ghaib (all that is hidden), none knows them but He. And He knows whatever there is in (or on) the earth and in the sea; not a leaf falls, but he knows it. There is not a grain in the darkness of the earth nor anything fresh or dry, but is written in a Clear Record." - Qur'ān, 6:59

Yet, He appoints angels to record our deeds—down to the finest details—so that justice may be upheld. Allāh refers to the angels as witnesses.

"Verily, We will indeed make victorious Our Messengers and those who believe (in the Oneness of Allāh Islāmic Monotheism) in this world's life and on the Day when the witnesses will stand forth, (i.e. Day of Resurrection)" - Qur'ān, 40:51

---

[10] Ṣaḥīḥ Muslim, Hadīth No. 131

On the Day of Judgment, there will be additional witnesses, including other eyewitnesses from mankind, and the one being judged himself as his body parts will bear witness against him. About mankind, the Qur'ān describes what the true believers will say,

"Our Lord! We believe in what You have sent down, and we follow the Messenger; so write us down among those who bear witness (to the truth i.e. Lā ilāha ill-Allāh – none has the right to be worshiped but Allāh)." - Qur'ān, 3:53

Other witnesses will be the Messengers sent to the people, as the Qur'ān says,

"....that the Messenger (Muhammad) may be a witness over you and you be witnesses over mankind!" - Qur'ān, 22:78

If the Creator of all that exists, Who is beyond anyone's command, is never unjust and calls witnesses to testify about things He already knows, it raises the question: *how can a human be unjust to another fellow human?* This serves as a profound lesson if only we would reflect on it.

While blatant injustice is definitely extreme, we learn that even when injustice is impossible, as Allāh is never unjust, there is still a strong need for a fair process. Indeed, all these are coupled with the fact that Allāh is not only the Most Just but also generously inclined to temper His justice with His boundless Mercy, which far outweighs His Wrath and anger.

Abū Huraira reported from the Messenger of Allāh (PBUH) who said,

"When Allāh completed the creation, He wrote in His book with Him upon the Throne: Verily, My mercy prevails over My wrath."[11]

The belief in angels, particularly the record-keepers, can help us become more patient and less reactive to injustices we face from others. In situations where oppression is severe and obtaining justice seems daunting—perhaps due to the oppressor's power or the absence of witnesses—a true believer finds comfort in knowing that there are unseen witnesses. Even if the oppressor escapes retribution in this imperfect world, they will face justice in the hereafter. The oppressed believer is assured that justice will be served, and the oppressor will receive their due punishment, or perhaps the believer will find some goodness and reward in the process, whether in this life, the next, or both.

This understanding can tame or even diminish the desire for revenge, as it brings solace to know that every wrong has been recorded and will be presented before the Most Competent Judge—the All-Powerful, the Ever-Just.

However, it's important to remember that the angels do not only record bad deeds; they are quick to log good ones, too, in contrast to their reluctance to record bad deeds. One might wonder why Allāh keeps this record. First, justice involves not just punishment but also rewarding good actions. Allāh's Will to punish for wrongdoing—while His Mercy supersedes His Wrath—indicates that He will also reward good, often in unexpected ways.

---

[11]Ṣaḥīḥ Muslim, Ḥadīth No 2751

We see this reflected in the Hadīth of the Prophet (PBUH) when he said,

"Having intercourse (with one's wife) is a charity." And the people said, "O Messenger of Allāh if one of us fulfills his desire, is there reward in that?" And he replied, "Do you not see that if he does it in a harām (unlawful) way, he will have the burden of sin? So if he does it in a halāl (lawful and permissible) way, he will have a reward for that."[12]

Secondly, Allāh periodically asks about the records of good deeds from the angels, even though He knows far better than they do. The Prophet (PBUH) said,

"There is no day when Allāh ransoms more people from the Fire than the day of 'Arafah.[13] He draws near, then He boasts about them to the angels and says, 'What do these people want?'"[14]

his statement serves as a lesson for us and an honor to be mentioned with love to the angels—those ever-obedient beings—even with all our imperfections.

In a more detailed narration, the Prophet (PBUH) said,

"Allāh, may He be blessed and exalted, has angels who travel about, with no other job but to seek out gatherings of dhikr (remembrance of Allāh). When they find a gathering in which

---

[12] Ṣaḥīḥ Muslim, Hadīth No. 1006

[13] 'Arafah is an important day in Islām that marks the completion of the Islāmic message and the Prophet Muhammad's (PBUH) farewell sermon. It occurs on the ninth day of Dhul-Hijjah, the last month of the Islāmic calendar, and is the second day of the Hajj pilgrimage in the holy city of Makkah in Saudi Arabia.

[14] Ṣaḥīḥ Muslim, Hadīth No. 1348

*Allāh is remembered, they sit with them and encircle them with
their wings until they fill the space between earth and the first
heaven. When they (the people) part, they (the angels) ascend to
heaven, and Allāh, may He be glorified and exalted, asks them,
although He knows best: 'From where have you come?' They say:
'We have come from some of Your slaves on earth, who were
glorifying You, magnifying You, proclaiming Your Oneness,
praising You, and asking of You.' He says: 'What are they asking
of Me?' They say: 'They are asking You for Your Paradise.' He
says: 'Have they seen My Paradise?' They say: 'No, O Lord.' He
says: 'So how about if they saw My Paradise?' They say: 'And they
are seeking Your protection.' He says: 'From what are they
seeking My protection?' They say: 'From Your Fire, O Lord.' He
says: 'Have they seen My Fire?' They say: 'No, O Lord.' He says:
'So how about if they saw My Fire?' They say: 'And they are asking
You for forgiveness.' He says: 'I have forgiven them, and given
them what they asked for, and granted them protection from that
from which they sought My protection.' They say: 'Lord, among
them is So and so, a sinner who was merely passing by, then he
sat with them.' He says: 'Him too I have forgiven. They are people
whose companion cannot be doomed.'"*[15]

These instances do not reflect Allāh seeking information; rather, they demonstrate His recognition of the remarkable virtues of these earthly beings before the angels,
serving as a form of honor. To spotlight their strong belief, Allāh points to their gatherings dedicated solely to
His remembrance, despite their limited understanding
of the true state of affairs. They request paradise, which
they have never seen, and seek protection from the hellfire,

---

[15] Ṣaḥīḥ Muslim, Ḥadīth No. 2689

which they have never experienced. Their genuine faith earns them both.

Allāh further displays His mercy when the angels inquire about a sinner among them. He responds that He has forgiven that sinner, stating He will never punish those who gather for His remembrance. In this way, Allāh honors humanity far beyond what they may deserve solely due to His Mercy. Such gatherings are encouraged, reminding believers that their actions are being witnessed. There is no greater motivation for righteous deeds than this.

In all of this, we see one of the angels' duties: to report our good deeds as soon as we perform them.

Narrated Abū Hurairah (RA): Allāh's Messenger (PBUH) said,

"(A group of) angels stay with you at night and (another group of) angels by daytime, and both groups gather at the time of the 'Asr and Fajr prayers. Then those angels who have stayed with you overnight ascend (to Heaven), and Allāh asks them (about you) - and He knows everything about you. "In what state did you leave My slaves?' The angels reply, 'When we left them, they were praying, and when we reached them they were praying.'"[16]

A believer who reads and reflects on this is more motivated to perform good deeds, especially knowing that angels are instantly recording their acts of kindness for Allāh. This awareness encourages them to do even more, as they understand that their good deeds are being recognized in a gathering far more exalted, even before the Day of Judgment.

---

[16] Ṣaḥīḥ al-Bukhārī 7429, Ḥadīth No. 56

08

CODIFYING THE STRAIGHT PATH – BELIEF IN HIS BOOKS

Iɴ the previous chapters, we explored how a lack of foundational beliefs can lead to confusion. We referred to these beliefs as *'Foundational Creed'*—certain beliefs and truths that guide our judgment. In Islām, this creed is firmly established, clearly documented, and free from alterations, adulterations, and confusion. Moreover, the Qur'ān, which codifies this Creed, carries a Divine promise to protect it from human flaws. Allāh says,

> *"Verily We: It is We Who have sent down the Dhikr (i.e. the Qur'ān) and surely, We will guard it (from corruption)."* -
> Qur'ān, 15:9

In many religions, there exists a flawed and ever-changing

set of beliefs, often with limited scope or, in some cases, no creed at all. This ambiguity allows both clergy and laity to modify their beliefs freely, altering their creeds to fit the shifting circumstances of life. Such improvisation inevitably leads to confusion. Religions that claim to stem from an 'unchangeable' God often find themselves in a state of constant flux, adapting to contemporary norms to the point where once-condemned sins become acceptable and even celebrated. Proponents of these evolving beliefs may call it progress, but true progress suggests that the original foundations were inadequate. *How, then, can you say that a defective set of beliefs—needing intellectual re-alignments—is from an infallible God who has full knowledge of Time and Space?*

While God may abrogate commandments in His Mercy to bring about something better for them as their situation changes, this is distinct from individuals making arbitrary amendments to suit their convenience. Human understanding is limited; thus, man-made religions are inherently unstable and susceptible to external influences. In contrast, Islām is clear and defined from its inception. Its core principles are straightforward and comprehensible, leaving no room for confusion. Adherents are guided on the straight path, striving to follow it to the best of their ability.

For those who seek truth, there is a continuous need to adhere to a reliable and universal standard. An unstable creed only breeds controversy and confusion among its followers. To avoid this, devotees must be able to discern right from wrong with certainty, relying on clear premises and sources that leave no room for doubt. This is why the

Qur'ān is a mercy for mankind.

"And We send down from the Qur'ān that which is a healing and a mercy to those who believe..." - Qur'ān 17:82

In their textual exegesis of this verse, the scholars of the Qur'ān point out that it addresses various ailments of the heart, such as "**doubt**, hypocrisy, shirk[1], **confusion** and an inclination towards falsehood."[2]

Islām promotes clarity by establishing belief in all the Books revealed by God through a select group of virtuous messengers throughout history. This ensures that no individual can suddenly claim divine revelation without basis, thus preventing a belief system that could lead to confusion among its followers.

Such a framework exposes the insincerity of those who may present themselves as 'Men of God,' allowing their deceptions to proliferate over time. Consequently, the uneducated may generalize all religions as mere tools for exploitation and control. It is very likely that many of those who hold this view have not truly considered Islām.

In Islām, even the Prophet (PBUH) is not granted the liberty to modify, add, or omit religious edicts arbitrarily at his own discretion.

One of the Prophet's wives, 'Āisha (R.A), narrated thus; The Prophet (PBUH) used to stay (for a period) in the house of Zainab bint Jahsh (another of his wives), and he used to drink honey in her house. Hafsah and I decided that when the Prophet (PBUH) entered upon either of us, she

---

[1]Shirk is an Arabic word for Polytheism
[2]Tafsīr Ibn Kathīr of Qur'ān, 17:82

would say, "I smell in you the bad smell of Maghāfir (a bad smelling raisin). Have you eaten Maghāfir?" When he entered upon one of us, she said that to him. He replied (to her), *"No, but I have drunk honey in the house of Zainab bint Jahsh, and I will never drink it again."*[3]

Then the following verse was revealed:

"O Prophet! Why do you ban (for yourself) that which Allāh has made lawful to you, seeking to please your wives? And Allāh is Oft-Forgiving, Most Merciful..." - Qur'ān, 66:1

Allāh admonishes the Prophet (PBUH) in this verse, reminding him that he cannot arbitrarily prohibit what is not forbidden. Without this clarification, Muslims might mistakenly believe that honey is forbidden. This spotlights Islām's reliance on divine guidance conveyed through the Prophet (PBUH). It's important to note that this verse was revealed to the Prophet (PBUH) himself, as he does not speak from his own volition.

"Your companion (Muhammad) has neither gone astray nor has erred. Nor does he speak of (his own) desire. It is only an Inspiration that is inspired. He has been taught (this Qur'ān) by one mighty in power [Jibrīl (Gabriel)]." - Qur'ān, 53:2-5

An Imām (a spiritual or religious leader) cannot un-expectedly claim to have received a divine command to abrogate or amend religious principles. Should he claim that the daily obligatory prayers should be six henceforth instead of the known five commanded by Allāh, he will

---

[3] Ṣaḥīḥ al-Bukhārī, Ḥadīth No. 6691

be required to provide acceptable proof (which he would not find outside the known sources); mere assertions of dreams or visions will not suffice or even count at all. His claims must be supported by the Qur'ān, the final revelation from God Almighty, the Sunnah of the Prophet Muhammad (PBUH), and the Ijmā'—the consensus of Islāmic scholars. To falsely invoke God's name is a serious matter that becomes very difficult to prove.

While there have been instances of individuals making outlandish claims of hearing from God, often coming forward to say God told them contradictory things about the same issue, Islām firmly codifies God's message, leaving little to no room for those who overstep their bounds and lie about divine communication.

There are four key aspects to the belief in Divine Revelation:

- Firm belief in the revealed Books of Allāh through His chosen Messengers.

- Recognition of these Books by their specific God-given and generic names.

- Acceptance of their contents, provided they remain unchanged, and based on the fourth aspect.

- Belief that Allāh revealed the Qur'ān as a witness—a quality control—over the other Books and to confirm them (in their original texts before they were tampered with by men.)

Allāh says,

"And We have sent down to you (O Muhammad) the Book (this Qur'ān) in truth, confirming the Scripture that came before it and Muhayminan (trustworthy in highness and a witness) over it (old Scriptures)." - Qur'ān, 5:48

This helps us understand the origins of other religions: Allāh sent Messengers to various communities with different revealed Books, ultimately delivering His final message—the Qur'ān—through Prophet Muhammad (PBUH). Following the death of these Messengers, some people deified them and turned to them in reverence and worship. No other religion provides as clear an explanation of how most religions were formed or came to be.

"It is not (possible) for any human being to whom Allāh has given the Book and Al-Hukma (the knowledge and understanding of the laws of religion, etc.) and Prophethood to say to the people: "Be my worshippers rather than Allāh's." On the contrary (he would say): "Be you Rabbāniyyūn (learned men of religion who practice what they know and also preach to others), because you are teaching the Book, and you are studying it." Nor would he order you to take angels and Prophets for lords (gods). Would he order you to disbelieve after you have submitted to Allāh's Will?" - Qur'ān, 3:79-80

To guard against corruption, the Qur'ān recounts stories from previous scriptures, discerning truths from falsehoods and guiding open hearts to the straight path. Allāh notes the consternation of the Jinn when they first encountered the Qur'ān,

"They said: "O our people! Verily! We have heard a Book (this Qur'ān) sent down after Musa (Moses), confirming what came before it, it guides to the truth and to a Straight Path (i.e. Islām)." - Qur'ān, 46:30

This occurred during a time when the Prophet of Islām, who was unlettered, had no access to these stories from earlier scriptures, much less the ability to translate them into Arabic or commit them to memory. This is just one of many signs that the Qur'ān is indeed from God Almighty.

The Prophet (PBUH) said,

"Every Prophet was given miracles because of which people believed, but what I have been given is the Divine Inspiration which Allāh has revealed to me. So I hope that my followers will outnumber the followers of the other Prophets on the Day of Resurrection."[4]

Self-Evidence and Authenticity

How do we establish that these claims about the Qur'ān are true?

First, the Qur'ān proves itself and demonstrates its own truth. Some might argue that a book cannot vouch for itself, but this argument is flawed. What is often mistaken for a book not proving itself is that a book cannot do so simply by saying it is correct. But there can be indications and signs that a book is correct, especially if it contains indisputable scientific, historical, mathematical, or philosophical facts that withstand the test of time. The Qur'ān is replete with such evidence.

---

[4] Ṣaḥīḥ al-Bukhārī, Hadīth No. 3

Consider a book on financial success: merely claiming to be the best in the market is not enough. However, your initial skepticism may wane if the principles it outlines are tried and tested in the business world. You might come to realize that the contents were, in fact, factual.

Conversely, if a book, claiming to be authored by God Almighty, is filled with contradictions, it would be difficult to accept, as God's words are eternally true, and contradictions imply falsehood. Additionally, if a book that has already proven itself in other matters further contains hidden knowledge of the universe that was impossible to know at the time—only just discovered scientifically within the last few years, using the most sophisticated cutting-edge technology—it would serve as another indicator of its divine origin. As expected and without any doubt, all of these qualities are abundantly present in the Qur'ān.

The Qur'ān boldly asserts its own inerrancy, claiming zero contradictions—a remarkable assertion that has remained true for over 1400 years. It says,

"Do they not then consider the Qur'ān carefully? Had it been from other than Allāh, they would surely have found therein much contradictions." - Qur'ān, 4:82

In this context, any objection to the Qur'ān's inerrancy must come from dissenters who dare challenge this assertion. However, since its divine revelation, we have found none, which stands as a significant sign. The Qur'ān also makes a similar bold claim regarding its divine immunity from any falsehood, being the words of the Magnificient, All-Knowing Diety.

"Falsehood cannot come to it from before it or behind it (it is) sent down by the All-Wise, Worthy of all praise" - Qur'ān, 41:42

We are yet to see any verse of the Qur'ān disproven, even by its most fervent enemies. If the Qur'ān were to invalidate a scientific position that was later confirmed, it would be a significant point. In fact, there are numerous instances where the Qur'ān has proven scientists wrong, which we will explore further in the next section. For now, it suffices to state unequivocally that despite the limits of human knowledge and the ever-changing theories of modern science, the Qur'ān remains unscathed, errorless, and free from falsehood.

The third point, an original book from God Almighty must contain knowledge that is clear-cut and exclusive to Him. The Qur'ān exemplifies this beautifully.

From the outset, the Qur'ān challenged its detractors—the unbelievers—to produce a book like it. Right from the onset, the Arabs, who prided themselves on their mastery of language and rhetoric, acknowledged the eloquence and brilliance of the Qur'ān when they heard it recited directly from the prophet (PBUH). Some, in their bewilderment, accused Prophet Muhammad (PBUH) of its authorship and false claims of a revelation. The holy prophet denies this, and perhaps it would have been easier and more prestigious for him if he had claimed the glory, saying all of this wisdom, eloquence, and miracles are from him. Maybe they would have worshiped him! Should that not be the goal of a liar? But through him, Allāh answered them in response,

"Or do they say: "He (Muhammad) has forged it (this Qur'ān)?" Nay! They believe not! Let them then produce a recital like unto it (the Qur'ān) if they are truthful." - Qur'ān, 52:33-34

Thus, the challenge remains unassailable: to produce something akin to the Qur'ān. The Arabs, with all of their scholarship and eloquence, alongside countless other deniers of the Qurān, have yet to succeed in this task, even to this day.

"Say: "If the mankind and the jinns (spirits) were together to produce the like of this Qur'ān, they could not produce the like thereof, even if they helped one another." - Qur'ān, 17:88

Here, Allāh states unequivocally how baseless the claim is that one man—Muhammad (PBUH)—authored the Qur'ān. No one has been able to replicate it, even with the assistance of all mankind and the Jinn. Allāh further refined the challenge, reducing it to replicating just a single chapter, yet no one has been able to provide a verse like it.

"And if you are in doubt concerning that which We have sent down (i.e. the Qur'ān) to Our slave (Muhammad), then produce a Surah (chapter) of the like thereof and call your witnesses besides Allāh, if you are truthful." - Qur'ān, 2:23

This relates to the Qur'ān's superiority as a divine revelation in terms of man's inability to produce something like it.

Now, what is something like it?

Only God Could Have Known

The Qur'ān uses signs in the Universe to point out that it can only be from God Almighty.

"We will show them Our Signs in the universe, and in their own selves, until it becomes manifest to them that this (Qur'ān) is the truth…" - Qur'ān, 41:53

First, the Qur'ān contains the knowledge that the study of the Universe and self will become a big deal with which people make judgments in later generations. The Qur'ān, written in 7th-century Arabia, contains numerous scientific facts that have only recently been discovered and confirmed using cutting-edge technology. Notably, it raises the question of how the Author of the Qur'ān knew that the universe would be studied in depth thousands of years later, a concept that was certainly not recognized in ancient times.

The civilization of 7th-century Arabia was far from sophisticated. Predominantly tribal during the time of Prophet Muhammad (PBUH), its culture highly valued oral traditions, as seen in its poetry, trade, and religious rituals. At that time, Arabs did not engage with astronomy systematically or scientifically. While they were somewhat familiar with constellations, this knowledge was passed down orally and primarily used for navigation during long journeys across scorching deserts and turbulent seas.

Astronomy only began to flourish among the Arabs long after the Qur'ān was revealed, serving as compelling evidence of its authenticity. The Qur'ān includes scientific assertions that could not have been understood with the primitive technology of that era. For example, it succinctly describes the stages of embryonic development, stating:

"And indeed We created man (Ādam) out of an extract of clay (water and earth). Thereafter We made him (the offspring of Ādam) as a Nutfah (mixed drops of the male and female sexual discharge) (and lodged it) in a safe lodging (womb of the woman). Then We made the Nutfah into a clot (a piece of thick coagulated blood), then We made the clot into a little lump of flesh, then We made out of that little lump of flesh bones, then We clothed the bones with flesh, and then We brought it forth as another creation. So blessed be Allāh, the Best of creators." - Qur'ān, 23:12-14

Professor Emeritus Keith L. Moore, One of the world's leading scientists in anatomy and embryology, stated: *"It is clear to me that these statements must have come to Muhammad from God because almost all of this knowledge was not discovered until many centuries later"*

Allāh also says in the Qur'ān,

"Have not those who disbelieve known that the heavens and the earth were joined together as one united piece, then We parted them? And We have made from water every living thing. Will they not then believe?" - Qur'ān, 21:30

Here, we find two distinct claims:

- first, that the heavens and the earth were once a single mass and

- second, that every living thing is primarily composed of or created from water.

From modern medicine, we confirm that the human body is composed of approximately 60 percent water on average.[5]. Water makes up 98 percent of all molecules in the bodies of livestock, and between 50 percent to 81 percent of an animal's body weight at maturity consists of water. to these animals, water is so vital that losing just 10 percent of body fluid can be fatal for most domestic livestock.[6]

A simple eye-gauge observation of animals and humans does not readily reveal this information. Surprisingly, an unlettered man in a distant corner of the world knew this over a thousand years ago! Such insights are neatly encapsulated in a single Book If Muhammad (PBUH) had been recognized for possessing such extraordinary eloquence and versatility, his people would not have been astonished by the Qur'ān.

A single verse in the Qur'ān suggests that the universe is expanding and that all living organisms are created from water. Only just discovered in the last few decades, it is evident that recent scientific theories align perfectly with the 1,400-year-old Qur'ān.

What kind of genius could have authored such profound knowledge while refusing to take full credit for it? Why would he deprive himself of that honor?

Another example relates to the sky. Simply put, the gases in the atmosphere act as a shield, protecting the Earth from the sun's deadly, hazardous rays. This phe-

---

[5] https://www.medicalnewstoday.com/articles/what-percentage-of-the-human-body-is-water

[6] Livestock Water Requirements (AS1763, Revised March 2021)

nomenon was only discovered by Joseph Fourier in 1824 and John Tyndall in 1859, who studied how the Earth's atmosphere traps heat, leading to the understanding of the greenhouse effect. Their findings reinforced the idea that the atmosphere plays a crucial role in maintaining Earth's temperature by shielding it from extreme solar radiation. Remarkably, this concept was mentioned in the Qur'ān over 1,400 years ago. It says,

"And We have made the heaven (open sky) a roof, safe and well guarded. Yet they turn away from its signs (i.e. sun, moon, winds, clouds, etc.)." - Qur'ān, 21:32

Consider the example of iron in its pure elemental metallic form. Scientists propose that such form of iron originates not from the Earth but from stars in the vastness of space. This discovery was made in the mid-20th century through the work of Hans Bethe and Fred Hoyle. Remarkably, the Qur'ān referenced this idea 1,400 years earlier, stating:

"...And We brought forth iron wherein is mighty power (in matters of war), as well as many benefits for mankind..." - Qur'ān, 57:25

How could an unlettered Arab in the remote Arabian desert possess such knowledge?

These examples barely scratch the surface of the many discoveries in modern science that are accurately described in the Qur'ān, undeniably pointing to the fact that it could only come from God.

Some may argue that such rare knowledge could have been sourced from various places. However, how did Muhammad (PBUH) discern and select only the accurate information, lifting only those **facts** that would later prove to be **true** in subsequent centuries?

09

SOMEONE TO FOLLOW –
BELIEF IN THE PROPHETS

I F Allāh had provided only commandments without a
practical model in the form of messengers and teach-
ers, some might dismiss these commands as impracti-
cal. Messages could easily be interpreted according to the
whims of would-be followers, leading to potential misinterpretations. However, with a prophet, a teacher, who
humanizes God's commands and exemplifies them, people are encouraged to emulate his example and strive to
live on the straight path.

Belief in God's Messengers—as vessels of Divine mercy
—is a fundamental aspect of the six Articles of Faith in
Islām. Allāh Almighty sent Messengers and Prophets to
convey divine messages to various peoples, with Prophet

Muhammad (PBUH) being the last and final prophet and messenger.

Allāh says,

"The Messenger (Muhammad) believes in what has been sent down to him from his Lord, and (so do) the believers. Each one believes in Allāh, His Angels, His Books, and His Messengers. They say, "We make no distinction between one another of His Messengers" - Qur'ān, 2:285

The verse above establishes the belief in the Messengers and refers to points we discussed in the previous chapter. In the Qur'ān, Allāh recounts the stories of His earlier messengers, using their mention to correct misguided beliefs associated with their names. Their inclusion sometimes affirms the enduring truths found in their earlier scriptures. Allāh says,

"And, indeed We have sent Messengers before you (O Muhammad); of some of them We have related to you their story..." - Qur'ān, 40:78

It is also important to emphasize here that these messengers were sent with similar and fundamentally identical messages.

"...Are the Messengers charged with anything but to convey clearly the Message?" - Qur'ān, 16:35

"And We did not send any Messenger before you (O Muhammad) but We inspired him (saying): Lā ilāha illā Ana [none has the right to be worshiped but I (Allāh)], so worship Me (Alone and none else)." - Qur'ān, 21:25

144

Their unity of purpose is reiterated in a Ḥadīth of Abū Hurayrah, wherein the Prophet Muhammad (PBUH) was quoted as saying:

"The Prophets are like brothers from one father, their mothers are different, but their religion is one"[1]

From their lives, we learn to persevere on the straight path. With practical and relatable examples, we draw inspiration from how Allāh strengthened Prophet Muhammad (PBUH) against his most formidable enemies. These avowed foes drove him from his homeland and pursued him across the scorching desert to the neighboring city of Madīnah, all in an attempt to extinguish the light of Islām and eliminate its early followers.We learn from this, yet another formidable lesson: we find strength in Allāh, for the Makkan forces, despite their superior firepower, faced a resolute wall against the Muslims and were decisively routed.

We also learn from the story of Prophet Ādam (PBUH) and the Angels about Allāh's deliberate intention in the creation of humanity.

"And (remember) when your Lord said to the angels: 'Verily, I am going to place (mankind) generations after generations on earth.' They said: 'Will You place therein those who will make mischief therein and shed blood, – while we glorify You with praises and thanks (Exalted be You above all that they associate with You as partners) and sanctify You?' He (Allāh) said: 'I know that which you do not know.'" - Qur'ān, 2:30

---

[1] Ṣaḥīḥ al-Bukhārī, Ḥadīth No. 3443

Everyone complied—except for Iblīs, who was arrogant—when Allāh commanded the Assembly of Angels to prostrate to Ādam. Iblīs (Satan), a Jinn[2], refused to bow, introducing the first known form of racism by claiming he was created from a superior substance, namely smokeless fire, in contrast to the inferior material—clay—used to create Ādam.

"(Allāh) said: 'What prevented you (O Iblīs) that you did not prostrate when I commanded you?' Iblīs said: 'I am better than him (Ādam), You created me from fire, and him You created from clay.' - Qur'ān 7:12

The lessons from this story become evidently relevant today, as the scourge of racism—manifested in today's widespread selective discrimination—undermines the very foundation of human unity.

From the tale of Ādam, we learn that humanity is inherently defective. The indiscretion of the first man—the father of mankind—reminds us to be less judgmental and more forgiving of others. We also learn that no child inherits the sins of their parents, contrary to the beliefs upheld by some religions. In Islām, we may inherit the blessings of Ādam but not his sins, reflecting Allāh's immense mercy.

Interestingly, in the Islāmic version of the Ādam story, his wife, did not entice him to sin. Thus, Muslims do not view women as the cause of man's downfall.

The Qur'ān not only contains inerrant information that no one could have been primed in at the time, but

---

[2]Iblīs was a Jinn not an Angel. Angels do not disobey Allāh but Jinns, like humans, are given free will.

it also emends on historical accounts that others supposed sources got wrong, setting the records straight. Perhaps, this is from the mercies of the Creator so that His message could be easily identified, leaving no chinks in the wall of truth, and no room for confusion.

Take the story of Noah's Ark, for example. At first glance, you will notice a handful of religious scriptures narrating the same story. Then, when you examine it clinically, you discover in this story a hidden code to identify which of the religious texts is authored by the Creator; one that remains inerrant, untampered with. God Almighty is Far above the limitations of Time and Space and, hence, makes no mistakes.

In the version reprised in the Bible, for example, it is claimed that the whole earth was submerged in the deluge, and only the fortunate few, walled off in the belly of the Ark, were saved. The problem, despondently, is that no evidence of a global flood has been found. According to scientific findings, there has been no global flood for over 10,000 years, just as there are many world regions that have remained desolate and dried for about a million years. Worse, the Bible sets an event time frame that falls within the period under review, where the cataclysmic misfortune was said to have happened.

When God Almighty sends a message that –in the passage of time – got tinkered with, it makes good sense to believe He will –out of His Bounties –eventually guide us through undeniable signs to parse truth from falsehood.

The version of this same story mentioned in the Qur'ān suggests a **localized** event, a flood only in a section of the known world, certainly **not global**. If the Qur'ān was a rehash of older books, the Bible specifically, how did an unlettered Arab know to parse facts from local legends, knowing precisely what to lift so his version does not contradict facts some 1,400 years later? Indeed these are signs for those sincerely seeking the truth.

Allāh is All-Wise and capable of all things, as illustrated in the story of Prophet Mūsā[3] (PBUH), who was marked for death by the tyrannical Pharaoh, Fir'aun[4]. Allāh did not only protect him, but allowed him to be raised in the Pharaoh's own household. This teaches us how defective and weak human plots can be; while man may plan, Allāh is the best of planners. We also learn that submitting our intellect to divine guidance on the straight path is far more powerful than relying on our own distorted logic. Abandoning a baby alone in the Nile during a desperate pursuit may seem illogical, yet it was the surest path to safety.

Another key lesson is that Allāh's Expansive Mercy encompasses all, even those whose hearts are most resistant to the truth. Pharaoh was called to salvation by Mūsā (PBUH) on Allāh's command, Who, while aware Pharaoh was not going to accept the message because He knows all things, still specifically instructed Mūsā (PBUH) to speak to him gently in calling him to guidance. Sadly, Pharaoh's heart was a lost cause.

"Go, both of you, to Fir'aun (Pharaoh), verily, he has transgressed (all bounds in disbelief and disobedience and behaved as an arrogant and as a tyrant). And speak to him

---

[3] Moses
[4] Pharaoh

mildly, perhaps he may accept admonition or fear Allāh."-
Qur'ān, 20:43-44

Allāh granted Prophet Mūsā (PBUH) several signs and wonders, such as his staff transforming into a living snake. Yet, despite these miracles, Pharaoh, who had requested a sign deepened his disbelief. From this, we learn that disbelief often stems from a deliberate rejection of the truth and that staunch disbelievers may refuse to believe, even when confronted with undeniable evidence.

"Truly! Those, against whom the Word (Wrath) of your Lord has been justified, will not believe. Even if every sign should come to them, – until they see the painful torment." - Qur'ān,
10:96-97

We also learn that we may never fully understand the wisdom behind Allāh's commands, as He knows best their ultimate outcomes. This is because while Fir'awn still did not believe, the sorcerers he called upon to contest Prophet Mūsā ended up believing, in contrast to Fir'aun's arrogance and disbelief.

"And the sorcerers fell down prostrate. They said: 'We believe in the Lord of the ʿĀlamīn (mankind, jinns and all that exists). The Lord of Mūsā (Moses) and Hārūn (Aaron).'" - Qur'ān,
7:120-122

We find similar lessons in the story of Prophet Ibrahim (PBUH), when he was commanded to sacrifice his only son, born to him in his old age. He did not hesitate, for he trusted his Lord's judgment, fully submitting to Him; he heard and obeyed. This command was a profound test for both father and son, and thankfully, they passed. Subsequently, Allāh replaced the dire command with another, substituting the son with an animal.[5]

"And, when he (his son) was old enough to walk with him, he said: "O my son! I have seen in a dream that I am slaughtering you (offer you in sacrifice to Allāh), so look what you think!" He said: "O my father! Do that which you are commanded, Inshā' Allāh (if Allāh will), you shall find me of As-Sābirīn (the patient ones, etc.)." Then, when they had both submitted themselves (to the Will of Allāh), and he had laid him prostrate on his forehead (or on the side of his forehead for slaughtering); And We called out to him: "O Abraham! You have fulfilled the dream (vision)!" Verily! Thus do We reward the Muhsinūn. Verily, that indeed was a manifest trial. And We ransomed him with a great sacrifice." - Qur'ān, 37:102–107

Today, we are not required to face the same extreme trials as tests of our faith, yet we often make lengthy excuses to stray from the straight path—especially those who do not reflect on these enlightening stories.

In the famous story of Prophet Yūsuf (PBUH), we admire how a young man, full of vitality, can resist the temptation of immoral advances. His story teaches us that physical beauty is not a license to indulge in sinful desires. There have been those before us, blessed with extraordinary beauty, who maintained their chastity.

---

[5] Interestingly, animals slaughtered as sacrifice in Islām are to be eaten by the people and given in charity, not left to waste like in fetish practices.

From the story of Prophet Ayyūb (PBUH), we learn the virtue of patience in the face of overwhelming adversity and misfortune. These examples abound, offering profound lessons.

Even in our daily lives, we can learn valuable lessons about family dynamics and manners. It's far better to follow the principles and examples set by these prophets than to navigate life's complexities in darkness, struggling to discern right from wrong. As mentioned earlier, seeking a new path on every issue can confuse us, regardless of our sincerity.

In mentorship, a mentee may not fully grasp the nuances of their mentor's guidance, even if they understand the broader context. The mentor, with greater experience and knowledge, provides insights born of lived experience. If this is true in human relationships, how much more so in our relationship with the Divine, the All-Knowing and Most Wise? Our response should be one of *"we hear and we obey,"* just as it is for His chosen Prophets.

The wisdom behind believing in the Prophets is multi-faceted. The wisdom for the general belief in the existence of Prophets are very numerous. That a Prophet was sent to every Nation challenges the very essence of racism as an antidote that is unparalleled. So, in every race and among every group of people, God Almighty found someone worthy enough to be His Messenger. It would not be understandable to a racist.

Some Prophets emerged from the lowest societal strata —downtrodden and poor—showing that God can elevate anyone from the depths. Not only were these Prophets exemplars of the best character and virtues, they were also surrounded by a brotherhood of moral integrity. This inspires individuals in any era or society to strive for improvement and become better than they were yesterday.

Having addressed the skepticism about God sending Prophets, how can we distinguish a true Prophet from a false one? The Jews reject the prophethood of 'Īsā ibn Maryam (Jesus) (PBUH), while Christians reject that of Muhammad (PBUH). As for Prophet 'Īsā (PBUH), the Qur'ān clarifies that he was a Prophet of Allāh and this should be believable because he had no role in the Qur'ān and did not even witness it. Furthermore, those who accuse Prophet Muhammad (PBUH) of fabricating the Qur'ān have no compelling reasons to explain why an Arab would confirm the teachings of a Jew. What benefit would that serve?

Ultimately, we are left with Prophet Muhammad's (PBUH) claim that the Qur'ān was revealed to him as a guide for humanity. Let us briefly consider how truly remarkable the prophethood of Muhammad (PBUH) is.

Why Not Just Claim It?

Assuming Prophet Muhammad (PBUH) was not sent by God Almighty, his impactful message still resonated with a vast segment of the population. *Why did not he choose to deify himself and seek worship from the people?* His community was steeped in idol worship, devoted to a pantheon of gods. They would have readily accepted such a tale, likely more than a call to servitude to the One True God. The former narrative would have easily captivated them.

Notably, at the outset of his ministry, it appeared as if his message might fizzle out over time—a perspective limited by human understanding. He faced tremendous challenges throughout his prophetic journey. Allāh acknowledges this, stating:

"Or think you that you will enter Paradise without such (trials) as came to those who passed away before you? They were afflicted with severe poverty and ailments and were so shaken that even the Messenger and those who believed along with him said, "When (will come) the Help of Allāh?" Yes! Certainly, the Help of Allāh is near!" - Qur'ān, 2:214

The entire chapter, Surat Ad-Duhā was revealed to console the Prophet (PBUH), saying,

"Your Lord (O Muhammad) has neither forsaken you nor hated you. And indeed the Hereafter is better for you than the present (life of this world). And verily, your Lord will give you (all i.e. good) so that you shall be well-pleased. Did He not find you (O Muhammad ()) an orphan and gave you a refuge? And He found you unaware (of the Qur'ān, its legal laws, and Prophethood, etc.) and guided you? And He found you poor, and made you rich (self-sufficient with self-contentment, etc.)?" - Qur'ān, 93:3-8

We find that it is not a case of a man who set out for the success his message later got. In fact, if we go back to the very beginning, we find him, anxiety etched on his face, asking his wife, Khadīja, *"Who will believe me?"* He was genuinely concerned. If this had been a scheme of his, he could have been sure enough of where he thinks he is going with it, and that would have been his motivation. instead, he was far from confident in any deceit.

Known Before Hand

Historically, even before he was called to prophetic duties, the Prophet Muhammad bin Abdullah (PBUH) was known as Al-Amīn, the trustworthy, among his peers in Makkah. Remarkably, he stood out for his virtues in a hedonistic society, never being recognized as a poet, writer, or intellectual. Yet, the most esteemed among the idolater Arabs of his time were in awe of the eloquence of the revealed Qur'ān. How did he manage this? How did he, seemingly out of nowhere, produce a recital that would forever shape the Arabic language? The depth of the Qur'ānic eloquence remains a phenomenon to this day. Consider the verse:

"And He it is Who has created the night and the day, and the sun and the moon, each in an orbit floating..." - Qur'ān, 21:33

The phrase *"each in an orbit,"*, written in Arabic, forms a palindrome—words that read the same, letter for letter, forward and backward. But it does not stop there; the sequence of these words in Arabic creates a loop akin to an orbit. How did an unlettered Arab put this together in his head and recited it out perfectly? Palindromes were not a common feature of early Arabic literary tradition.

In fact, Arabic palindromes only became prevalent in later periods, particularly during the Islāmic Golden Age (8th to 14th centuries), when arts, science, and literature flourished. The Qur'ān would have lost its linguistic impact on the Arabs if Muhammad (PBUH), its proponent, had been recognized as a literary expert—yet he was not.

It is also important to note his reputation for trustworthiness. Called to prophethood at the age of 40, in the prime of his life, he had spent his entire existence among his people, who could attest to his character.

It is essential to recognize that times were different; people did not easily pretend to be someone they were not. Life was more straightforward, and individuals were generally more sincere. Even today, a 40-year-old raised in a close-knit community is well-known to his peers.

So, how much more so then? His community knew him as a trustworthy man. It makes no logical sense for such a person to suddenly change based on a strange recital attributed to a Creator to whom he is wholly subservient in worship. It simply does not add up.

How Did He "Copy" Only the Correct Things?

In light of the many undeniable evidences in the Qur'ān that underscore its authorship by God Almighty, some have carelessly suggested that certain passages were simply borrowed from earlier texts. Unfortunately for proponents of this argument, they cannot explain how an unlettered man could discern accurate information from fabrications, selectively appropriating only the valid content.

How come he only copied the science-related hypotheses that were right? How did he know which was wrong so that he did not add it to the Qur'ān?

This simply implies a level of discernment that brings the argument back to square one.

Historically, there was a belief that human babies were born as blank slates, a theory that persisted until 1684. However, this notion has since been completely disproven by more advanced evidence that aligns perfectly with the Qur'ānic perspective, which asserts that human babies are not blank at birth.

"And by Nafs[6], and Him Who perfected him in proportion; Then He showed him what is wrong for him and what is right for him; Indeed he succeeds who purifies his ownself (i.e. obeys and performs all that Allāh ordered, by following the true Faith of Islāmic Monotheism and by doing righteous good deeds). And indeed he fails who corrupts his ownself." - Qur'ān, 91:7-10

From the above, we can deduce that humans possess innate tendencies toward both good and evil. In another verse, an oppressor of the praying Muslims is reproached as follows:

"Nay! If he (Abū Jahl) ceases not, We will catch him by the forelock. A lying, sinful forelock!" - Qur'ān, 96:15-16

In the verse above, many have observed that Allāh may be alluding to the role of the prefrontal cortex in the human brain, particularly in actions like lying. This aligns with the insights revealed in the verse.

The crucial point is that Allāh acknowledges an inherent propensity for both good and evil within humans. It is remarkable that the Prophet Muhammad (PBUH) did not endorse the widely accepted notion of humans as blank slates, despite its prevalence among intellectuals of his time.

---

[6]This word generally means Soul

What more signs do people need?

Why the Humility?

The Prophet Muhammad (PBUH) instructed us to pray for him, teaching us to say, *"Allāhumma salli alā Muhammadin, wa alā āli Muhammadin"*[7] which translates to *"O Allāh, send Your grace, honor, and mercy upon Muhammad and his family."*

Given the wonders of the Qur'ān, it might seem fitting for him to claim divinity and attract a large following. However, he humbly acknowledged his role as a servant and messenger of God. He said,

> *"By Allāh, I seek forgiveness from God and repent to Him more than seventy times a day."*[8]

As mentioned in an earlier chapter, there was a time when some of his wives made him believe the honey he ingested had a bad smell, leading to his self-reprimand when he forbade himself from consuming it. Allāh corrected him that he cannot forbid what Allāh has not forbidden.

Throughout the Qur'ān, the Prophet (PBUH) faced correction for various actions like when he turned away from an innocent inquirer in discomfort, Allāh corrected him. There was another time he made supplications after the Battle of Uhud[9] when he was injured and lost a tooth. He was asking Allāh's wrath to descend on some of those indi-

---

[7] Ṣaḥīḥ al-Bukhārī, Book 79, Hadīth 80
[8] Ṣaḥīḥ Al-Bukhārī, Hadīth 319
[9] The Battle of Uhud (625 CE) was sparked by those who attacked the Prophet before seeking revenge for their defeat leading to a clash near Medina where a Muslim strategic error resulted in a setback.

viduals who had caused him pain and Allāh revealed that he had no command or authority over their affairs. Interestingly, some of those he prayed against later embraced Islām, becoming great believers and role models.

On another occasion, he rejected a companion's suggestion, only to be later revealed through divine guidance that the suggestion was indeed the better option. Similarly, when he provided his own opinion on a worldly matter, a companion asked if it was a revelation or his own thought. The Prophet (PBUH) clarified it was from him, and when the companion offered a contrary opinion, the Prophet (PBUH) appreciated it.

Allāh, at some point, prevented him from having any more wives and all of these conveyed through the same blessed book and through his own speech.

Such humility and self-effacement are rare traits in those who fabricate stories or claim prophethood. Once, he reproached a man who knelt to greet him, asserting that only Allāh deserves such worship. This level of humility is truly exceptional.

"Your companion (Muhammad) has neither gone astray nor has erred. Nor does he speak of (his own) desire. It is only an Inspiration that is inspired. He has been taught (this Qur'ān) by one mighty in power [Jibrīl (Gabriel)]." - Qur'ān, 53:2-5

10

Self-Check with a Schedule – Belief in the Day of Judgment

IT is often said that an unexamined life is not worth living, a notion that can feel cliché. Yet, *how does a person who is comfortable with their position in life find the motivation to examine or even reflect on it?* We frequently hear about Karma—reaping what you sow.

But what about those who witness wrongdoers escaping justice while the virtuous suffer? How can people then maintain faith in the principle of Karma?

Islām makes it an Article of Faith, a fundamental tenet, to believe that there exists a Day of Judgment. On that day, every deed, big or small, will be laid bare, and individuals will account for their actions. Those who have genuinely done good will receive their due rewards, even if they were overlooked in this life. Conversely, those who engage in evil will face their reckoning—except for those who sincerely repent and are forgiven.

"And surely, the Hour is coming, there is no doubt about it..." - Qur'ān, 22:7

Mankind will be gathered and brought together, and even the dead and decayed will be resurrected—bone by bone, imperfection and all—by Allāh. Regarding this resurrection, He says:

"Thereof (the earth) We created you, and into it, We shall return you, and from it, We shall bring you out once again." - Qur'ān, 20:55

This must happen so that everyone can face judgment and give account for their deeds. Allāh says:

"Then they are returned to Allāh, their Maulā [True Master (God), the Just Lord (to reward them)]. Surely, His is the Judgment, and He is the Swiftest in taking account." - Qur'ān, 6:62

For those who doubt or believe it impossible for a decayed body, aged and reduced to dust, to be restored to life—every part reassembled—Allāh says:

"Does man (a disbeliever) think that We shall not assemble his bones? Yes, We are Able to put together in perfect order the tips of his fingers (fingerprints). Nay! (Man denies Resurrection

and Reckoning. So) he desires to continue committing sins.” -
Qur'ān, 75:3-5

The Qur'an mentions how Allāh reassembles all human body parts, even down to the intricacies of fingerprints. Some may ask why fingerprints were an emphasis when they were a non-issue at the time. However, the Qur'ān is no ordinary book; it is a clear revelation from the Almighty.

Importantly, judgment will be based on a balanced scale. This reflects the beauty of Islām and the mercy of Allāh, who recognizes our innate tendency to sin while urging us to repent. Some sins may slip through, for which we did not repent or whose repentance was not accepted.

Yet, these sins will not lead their perpetrators to hell-fire. Instead, they will be weighed against their good deeds. Ultimately, a person is deemed successful if their good deeds outweigh their sins.

“Then as for him whose balance (of good deeds) will be heavy, he will live a pleasant life (in Paradise). But as for him whose balance (of good deeds) will be light, he will have his home in Hāwiyah (pit, i.e. Hell).” - Qur'ān, 101:6-9

The scale, as outlined, will leave out no detail. Remember Allāh's statement when He said:

“So whosoever does good equal to the weight of an atom (or a small ant), shall see it. And whosoever does evil equal to the weight of an atom (or a small ant) shall see it.” - Qur'ān, 99:7-8

The above is coupled with the angels' hesitation to document bad deeds, as Allāh has decreed this out of His mercy. However, a believer should neither trivialize their sins nor despair of Allāh's mercy. Abdullah ibn Mas'ūd (RA), a companion of the Prophet Muhammad (PBUH) captured it correctly when he said,

"The believer sees his sins as if he is sitting at the foot of a mountain, fearing it might fall on him, while the sinner (fājir) views his sins as a fly landing on his nose, which he simply waves away."[1]

Even with a mountain of sins, the believer must not lose hope in the mercies of Allāh.

"Say: 'O 'Ibādi (My slaves) who have transgressed against themselves (by committing evil deeds and sins)! Despair not of the Mercy of Allāh, verily Allāh forgives all sins. Truly, He is Oft-Forgiving, Most Merciful.'" - Qur'ān 39:53

Allāh will forgive in this world, just as He will, away from prying eyes, inform others of His forgiveness. Indeed, He is Most Merciful!

Afterward, people are either admitted to Paradise or cast into Hellfire—each according to their deeds.

"Verily, those who believe and do righteous good deeds, they are the best of creatures. Their reward with their Lord is 'Adn (Eden) Paradise (Gardens of Eternity), underneath which rivers flow, they will abide therein forever..." - Qur'ān, 98:7-8

"They who disbelieve and deny our Āyāt (proofs, evidences, verses, lessons, signs, revelations, etc.) are those who will be the dwellers of the Hell-fire." - Qur'ān, 5:10

---

[1] Jami' at-Tirmidhī 2497

The Day of Judgment will be the most daunting and demanding day of our entire existence. Belief in its imminence is meant to reform us and deepen our God-consciousness. The Qur'ān says:

"O mankind! Fear your Lord and be dutiful to Him! Verily, the earthquake of the Hour (of Judgment) is a terrible thing." - Qur'ān, 22:1

"When the heaven is cleft asunder. And when the stars have fallen and scattered; and when the seas are burst forth. And when the graves are turned upside down (and they bring out their contents)..." - Qur'ān, 82:1-4

The Prophet (PBUH) said about this expected Day,

"The feet of the son of Adam will not move from before his Lord on the Day of Judgment until he is asked about five things: his life and how he lived it, his youth and how he used it, his wealth and how he earned and spent it, and how he acted upon what he acquired of knowledge."

A true believer, having reflected on these truths and firmly believing in the Day of Accountability, will find themselves better prepared for all four of these aspects. They will be motivated to prioritize their efforts for the Hereafter over worldly pursuits. They will heed the words of the Prophet (PBUH), who reminds them that they are mere passers-by in this life, as commonly expressed, *'life is transient.'* They will feel a deeper concern if they falls short of pleasing Allāh. The Qur'ān says:

"Say (O Muhammad): "Verily, my Salāt (prayer), my sacrifice, my living, and my dying are for Allāh, the Lord of the ʿĀlamīn (mankind, jinns and all that exists)." - Qurʾān, 6:162

The Prophet (PBUH) spoke about the dangers of being overly focused on worldly life,

"Whoever focuses all his concerns on one issue, which is the concern of the Hereafter, Allāh will suffice him and spare him the worries of this world. But whoever wanders off in concerns over different worldly issues, Allāh will not care in which of these valleys he is destroyed."[2]

Indeed, Allāh is sufficient for those who stand with Him, and this support is not limited to the Hereafter. He says:

"Is not He (better than your gods) Who responds to the distressed one, when he calls Him, and Who removes the evil, and makes you inheritors of the earth, generations after generations. Is there any ilāh (god) with Allāh? Little is that you remember!" - Qurʾān 27:62

It can be inferred from the above that whoever focuses on the Hereafter, Allāh will ease their worldly affairs. However, it is important to note that Allāh's ease may not always align with human notions of success. Some may appear successful yet find no true tranquility. Ultimately, no matter the circumstances, Allāh assists believers in achieving their ultimate goal: peace of mind through unity with the

---

[2] Sunan Ibn Mājah, Hadīth No. 257

Divine and contentment even with minimal material resources, as human desires are insatiable.

An example was given when Huthayfah (RA) said:

"Whenever the Prophet (PBUH) was grieved by a thing, he used to offer (al-Salāt) the prayers."[3]

This should be coupled with the Prophet's (PBUH) exhortation to *'tie your camel and then trust in Allāh.'* We must engage in our worldly affairs, as these principles do not prevent us from striving or competing within the boundaries set by Allāh. However, we should not let worldly gains overshadow our focus on the Hereafter. Our primary attention should be directed toward Allāh. He says:

"O you who believe! Fear Allāh and keep your duty to Him. And let every person look to what he has sent forth for the morrow, and fear Allāh. Verily, Allāh is All-Aware of what you do." - Qur'ān, 59:18

The consequences of placing too high a value on this worldly life while neglecting the Hereafter are a troubled mind filled with depression and immense distress. Allāh says:

"...then whoever follows My Guidance shall neither go astray, nor fall into distress and misery. But whosoever turns away from My Reminder (i.e. neither believes in this Qur'ān nor acts on its orders, etc.) verily, for him is a life of hardship, and We shall raise him up blind on the Day of Resurrection." - Qur'ān, 20:123-124

---

[3] Sunan Abī Dāwūd, Hadīth No. 1319

For the believer who strives—through ease and hardship—to please their Lord and Creator, living with the Day of Judgment in mind resembles the concept of delayed gratification. In contrast, those who are indifferent to the Hereafter and live on autopilot, driven by whims as vast as Everest, are warned by Allāh:

"Whoever wishes for the quick-passing (transitory enjoyment of this world), We readily grant him what We will for whom We like. Then, afterwards, We have appointed for him Hell, he will burn therein disgraced and rejected, (far away from Allāh's Mercy)." - Qur'ān, 17:18

We must also understand that 'there are levels to this.' Some will be at ease and confident on the Day of Judgment, while others will face fear yet receive good news. Still others, with grief etched on their faces, will hear bad news. Humanity will traverse the Bridge of Sirat, sharp as a blade and difficult to cross. The Prophet (PBUH) said:

"There will be people who will cross the Sirat as quickly as the blink of an eye, others as fast as lightning, the wind, fast horses, or camels. Some will be safe without any harm; some will be safe after receiving some scratches, and some will fall into Hell."[4]

This point is crucial, as even among believers, some may do less good, considering certain evils inconsequential and indulging in them freely. A believer must strive not only to succeed on the Day of Judgment but to attain the highest ranks, making their ordeal much easier.

---

[4] Saḥīḥ al-Bukhārī, Hadīth No. 7439

For example, the Day will commence with an extended period of standing, aptly named the Day of Standing. This standing will endure for a long time, filled with immense hardship and pervasive fear. Imagine the dread of being cast into the fire, holding one's breath as they ponder their fate. This is just one aspect of the Day's trials—a day when there will be no shade from the scorching sun. However, the Prophet (PBUH) told us that some will find solace under the shade, a much-needed respite. He further elaborated on the seven categories of people who will enjoy this privilege, saying:

"There are seven whom Allāh will shade with His shade on the day when there will be no shade except His: the just ruler; a young man who grows up worshiping his Lord; a man whose heart is attached to the mosque; two men who love one another for the sake of Allāh and meet and part on that basis; a man who seduced by a woman of rank and beauty and says 'I fear Allāh'; a man who gives in charity and conceals it to such an extent that his left-hand does not know what his right hand gives; and a man who remembers Allāh when he is alone, and his eyes fill up."[5]

Is there any better reason for a true believer to strive to be among these categories? If a billion people today genuinely aimed for these ideals, the world would undoubtedly be a better place. Imagine if one in every seven individuals sought to be a Just Ruler, a disciplined young person devoted to worship, someone who meets others based on principles, gives charity in secret, or reflects on the

---

[5] Ṣaḥīḥ Al-Bukhārī, Hadīth No. 629

wonders of Creation to the point of tears. Many positive changes would naturally follow.

From this belief—reiterated in previous chapters—we learn that Allāh is most Just. He allows witnesses even when His all-encompassing Knowledge is sufficient. Regarding the Day of Judgment, Allāh is not compelled to designate a Day for judgment; He is fully aware of everything that has transpired and is answerable to no one. Yet, He establishes justice by granting everyone a fair hearing. A person who reflects on this might hold himself accountable for his injustices toward others, recognizing how just Allāh is with us, even without needing to be. He created us, owns us, and everything that exists. Concerning this, Allāh says:

"And We shall set up balances of justice on the Day of Resurrection, then none will be dealt with unjustly in anything. And if there be the weight of a mustard seed, We will bring it. And Sufficient are We as Reckoners." - Qur'ān 21:47

It was narrated that Jābir said: When the emigrants who had crossed the sea came back to the Messenger of Allāh, he said: *"Why do not you tell me of the strange things that you saw in the land of Ethiopia?"* Some young men among them said: "Yes, O Messenger of Allāh. Whilst we were sitting, one of their elderly nuns came past, carrying a vessel of water on her head. She passed by some of their youths, one of whom placed his hand between her shoulders and pushed her. She fell on her knees, and her vessel broke. When she stood up, she turned to him and said: *'You will come to know, O traitor, when Allāh sets up the Footstool and gathers the first and the last, and hands and feet speak of what they used to earn. You will come to know how you and I stand before Him.'"* The Messenger of Allāh then said:

"She spoke the truth, she spoke the truth. How can Allāh purify any people (of sin) when they do not support their weak and oppressed ones against the strong?"[6]

The balance of recompense and retribution on the Day of Judgment makes the concept of reincarnation unnecessary. What is the logic in being reincarnated as a poor person as a form of justice for having stolen from the poor in a past life? Allāh will compensate the poor for their losses and administer appropriate punishment for the theft.

This brings us to another important point: the rights of others. Those who harm others in sin will have their good deeds taken away and given as reparation to their victims. If their good deeds are insufficient or depleted, the bad deeds of their victims will be added to their account.

This balancing act provides solace to the wronged. There is a silver lining to their patient suffering; they may earn more good deeds or have some of their sins transferred. Often, we lack the patience to endure gracefully, resorting to backbiting our oppressors and further diminishing our own goodness.

We must remember that even though the Day of Judgment is a day of accountability, Allāh's promise to His believing servants holds true and will not be suspended. Allāh says:

---

[6] Sunan Ibn Mājah, Hadīth No. 4010. Classed as hasan by al-Albāni in Ṣaḥīḥ Sunan Ibn Mājah, 3255

"...and it will be a hard Day for the disbelievers" - Qur'ān 25:26

"Truly, that Day will be a Hard Day. Far from easy for the disbelievers." - Qur'ān, 74:9-10

Scholars interpret these two verses as a promise of ease and comfort for believers on the Day of Judgment. It is the arrogant persistence in sin that may lead to a person's downfall, resulting in immense discomfort. A believer must avoid immoral actions that are characteristic of the people of Hellfire, as highlighted throughout the Qur'ān and Hadīth.

"O you who believe! Eat not Ribā (usury or interest) doubled and multiplied, but fear Allāh that you may be successful. And fear the Fire, which is prepared for the disbelievers. And obey Allāh and the Messenger (Muhammad) that you may obtain mercy. And march forth in the way (which leads to) forgiveness from your Lord, and for Paradise as wide as are the heavens and the earth, prepared for Al-Muttaqūn (the pious)" - Qur'ān 3:130-133

We learn here of several actions to avoid in order to be saved from the Hellfire. In the next verse, we see that denying the Day of Judgment is a certain path to the fire.

"About Al-Mujrimūn (polytheists, criminals, disbelievers, etc.), (And they will say to them): 'What has caused you to enter Hell?' They will say: 'We were not of those who used to offer their Salāt (prayers), nor we used to feed Al-Miskīn (the poor); And we used to talk falsehood (all that which Allāh hated) with vain talkers. And we used to belie the Day of

Recompense, until there came to us (the death) that is
certain.'" - Qur'ān, 74:41-47

One significant aspect of denying the Day of Recompense (the Day of Judgment) or an outright refutation of its existence, is that it causes a person to cease being a Muslim. Another aspect is ignoring its importance, allowing it to carry little weight in the regular evaluation of our deeds. Living as if we will not be held accountable for our actions means succumbing to our insatiable desires instead of striving to do what is right.

When a believer abstains from major sins and does not justify minor ones—rather, he works to avoid them while constantly seeking repentance—Allāh grants him glad tidings of success in ways he may never have imagined.

"No person knows what is kept hidden for them of joy as a
reward for what they used to do." - Qur'ān, 32:17

And Allāh says in a Hadīth Qudsī:

"I have prepared for My righteous slaves that which no eye has
seen, no ear has heard nor has it entered the heart of man."[7]

There are a few pleasures in this worldly life that may bear some distant resemblance to Allāh's promises in Paradise, as mentioned in the verse. However, no mortal can truly quantify or draw adequate parallels to what Allāh has prepared for the righteous servant.

From 'Ubādah ibn As-Sāmit (RA), the Prophet (PBUH) who said:

---

[7] Ṣaḥīḥ Al-Bukhārī, Hadīth No. 7498

"Whoever loves to meet Allāh, Allāh will love to meet him, and whoever hates to meet Allāh, Allāh will hate to meet him." 'Aishah (RA) or one of his wives said: "But we all dislike the idea of death." He said, "It is not what you are thinking. When death approaches the believer, and he is given the news of Allāh's pleasure and honor, nothing will be dearer to him than what lies ahead of him, so he will love to meet Allāh, and Allāh will love to meet him. But when death approaches the disbeliever, and he is given the news of Allāh's wrath and punishment, nothing will be more disliked by him than what lies ahead of him, so he will hate to meet Allāh, and Allāh will hate to meet him."[8]

Hope for the Hopeless

Belief in the Day of Judgment serves as a security and a buffer against harsh self-criticism and societal judgment. Without it, we might commit evil recklessly and unfairly assess ourselves. This is reflected in a Hadīth where a person comes before Allāh on the Day of Judgment, believing—by his own flawed assessment—that he is undeserving of mercy. Allāh, however, reminds him of his good deeds, as a way of ultimately saying, We are not Unaware of them, before pardoning him.[9]

We often judge ourselves harshly, feeling condemned for our mistakes. This belief teaches us that our self-assessment may be too severe and that no one truly attains success on that Day except by the Mercy of Allāh.

For others, they may have committed grave sins that society refuses to forget, labeling them as irredeemable.

---

[8] Ibn Mājah, Hadīth No. 4264
[9] Ṣaḥīḥ Al-Bukhārī Hadīth No. 6070, and No. 2441

Despite knowing the circumstances that led them astray and their efforts to reform themselves, society's judgment can be unrelenting. Even when they have changed and returned to righteousness, they might still feel burdened by the stigma of past misdeeds.

Understanding that society's judgment is not the final word offers solace. Man's judgment often condemns us indefinitely, even after we have repented and made amends. But Allāh's judgment is different; He recognizes growth, reformation, and repentance. He rewards these efforts, replacing our bad deeds with good, as symbolized by the scales on the Day of Judgment.

Allāh says:

"Except those who repent and believe (in Islāmic Monotheism), and do righteous deeds, for those, Allāh will change their sins into good deeds, and Allāh is Oft-Forgiving, Most Merciful." - Qur'ān 25:70

Perhaps things may worsen because of your past mistakes. However, belief in the Day of Judgment means accepting that, despite the consequences of your bad decisions in this world, there is always the possibility for redemption as long as you are alive. It reminds us that the Day of Accountability has not yet arrived, offering hope for personal rectitude and transformation. It also helps us place human judgment in its proper context—on the periphery—because we know that people do not have the final say.

This understanding is crucial because humans, except when guided by faith, can be unforgiving. People may speak of forgiveness on small matters, but when hurt runs deep, forgiveness often escapes their wounded hearts. This, however, is not the case with God Almighty.

Narrated Abū Saʿīd Al-Khudrī, the Prophet (PBUH) said,

"Amongst the men of Bani Israel, there was a man who had murdered ninety-nine persons. Then he set out asking (whether his repentance could be accepted or not). He came upon a monk and asked him if his repentance could be accepted. The monk replied in the negative, and so the man killed him. He kept on asking till a man advised him to go to such and such village. (So, he left for it) but death overtook him on the way. While dying, he turned his chest towards that village (where he had hoped his repentance would be accepted). So, the angels of mercy and the angels of punishment quarreled amongst themselves regarding him. Allāh ordered the village (towards which he was going) to come closer to him and ordered the village (whence he had come), to go far away. Then He ordered the angels to measure the distances between his body and the two villages. So, he was found to be one span closer to the village (he was going to). So, he was forgiven."[10]

Allāh, the All-Powerful, could have simply decreed that the man died in the land of repentance, but He chose to tilt the earth in his favor, highlighting how much He values repentance and loves when we change our ways. Even though this man had no chance to perform good deeds after repenting, Allāh still tipped the scales in his favor.

---

[10] Ṣaḥīḥ Al-Bukhārī, Ḥadīth No. 676 and Ṣaḥīḥ Muslim, Ḥadīth No. 2766

What crime have you committed that shakes your heart, makes you feel irredeemable, or grants society the unwarranted right to condemn you forever?

All you need is sincere repentance and genuine effort to turn a new leaf and do what is right. Allāh loves that you are striving to improve, and you will be amazed at how much this effort weighs on your scale.

Abū Hurairah (May Allāh be pleased with him) reported that the Messenger of Allāh (PBUH) said,

"Allāh says: 'I am just as My servant thinks of Me when he remembers Me.' By Allāh! Allāh is more pleased with the repentance of His servant than one of you who unexpectedly finds in the desert his lost camel. 'He who comes closer to Me one span, I come closer to him a cubit; and he who comes closer to Me a cubit, I come closer to him a fathom; and if he comes to Me walking, I come to him running". [11]

"Nay, you prefer the life of this world; although the Hereafter is better and more lasting."—Qur'ān, 87:16-17

---

[11] Ṣaḥīḥ al-Bukhārī, Hadīth No 7405 and Ṣaḥīḥ Muslim, Hadīth No 2675

11

IT IS NOT IN YOUR HANDS –
THE BELIEF IN DESTINY

MUCH has been said about the fear of the unknown and how it paralyzes people, holding them back. You might find a person who intends a good, but is scared stiff. He investigates why, only to discover the uncertainty of the outcome unnerves him. Now, let us talk about a Belief system that is comfortable with helpless feelings of uncertainty. One that finds ease in knowing we might never know where we are headed, even if we have to play our part within a vacuum of knowledge. Allāh says about predestination,

"Verily, We have created all things with Qadar (predestination)." - Qur'ān, 54:49

For many, the most challenging aspect of believing in God is reconciling His existence with the presence of evil. This dilemma often provokes strong reactions from those who rely on human logic to interpret religion, leading them to deny God's foreknowledge of evil. They may attribute all evil to the Devil, implying that God is either oblivious to it or that evil occurs outside His will. This view is fundamentally inaccurate and erroneous. While Allāh holds no responsibility for any malicious intent and its consequences, He permits them to exist; otherwise, they would not come to pass. As He states:

"No calamity befalls on the earth or in yourselves but is inscribed in the Book of Decrees (Al-Lauh Al-Mahfūz), before We bring it into existence. Verily, that is easy for Allāh." - Qur'ān, 57:22

No one can overpower Allāh or act against His will; He is All-Powerful. He has the authority to prevent anything from occurring. Allāh allows certain evils to show us we have free will, having clearly shown the path of right and wrong; with it, a person might steer their own barge and choose their own path, enabling them to navigate their own choices, even though the outcomes of those choices are already known to Him.

Additionally, what we often perceive as evil in a human context may not be truly evil from a Divine perspective. Not everything we see as bad is bad, neither is everything we hate bad for us.

"...and it may be that you dislike a thing which is good for you and that you like a thing which is bad for you. Allāh knows but

you do not know." - Qur ān, 2:216

Allāh may decree that a person loses 3 of their children. Crushing as this will be on a parent, spelling the end of their world, knowing that Allāh owns us—and, by extension, all that we own—we are comforted, helping to ease the accompanying pain.

A Muslim understands that a child is a precious gift from Allāh, and it is within His power to take that gift back at any moment, often without warning.

The Prophet (PBUH) said:

". . . whatever Allāh takes is His, and whatever He gives is His, and everything with Him has a limited fixed term (in this world)..."[1]

It might be that Allāh intended to guarantee their success. The Prophet (PBUH) said,

"When a person's child dies, Allāh says to His angels, 'You have taken the child of My slave.' They say, 'Yes.' He says, 'You have taken the apple of his eye.' They say, 'Yes.' He says, 'What did My slave say?' They say, 'He praised you and said "Innā lillahi wa innā ilayhi raji'ūn (Verily to Allāh we belong and unto Him is our return).' Allāh says, 'Build for My slave a house in Paradise and call it the house of praise.'"[2]

It is important to note that the grand edifice being built in their names in Paradise is often referred to, in our limited understanding, as 'a house.' The world's most

---

[1] Ṣaḥīḥ Bukahrī, Hadīth No. 7377
[2] Sunan al-Tirmidhī, No. Hadīth 1021

beautiful house pales compared to anything in Paradise. Imagine the joy such a person will experience in these eternal provisions—only Allāh knows the full extent of their enjoyment and purpose.

Consider, too, that the same child may be admitted to Paradise, where they will dwell in everlasting tranquility. *So, how significant are our worldly sorrows, really?* If we endure with fortitude and patience, we can look forward to a reward beyond this life. He (PBUH) also said:

"Any woman who loses three of her children, they will be a shield for her against the Fire." A woman said, "And two?" He said, "And two."[3]

In another narration, he specifically addresses those who have lost young children, stating:

"There is no Muslim who loses three of his children before they reach the age of puberty, but Allāh will admit him to Paradise by virtue of His Mercy towards them."[4]

Losing a child is often regarded as one of the most devastating experiences a parent can face. Fortunately, there is a reassuring promise; He (PBUH) says:

"There is no Muslim who is afflicted with a calamity and says that which Allāh has enjoined, Innā lillāhi wa innā ilayhi raji'ūn. Allāhumma ajirnī fī musībatī wakhluf lī khayran minhā (Verily to Allāh we belong and unto Him is our return. O Allāh, reward me for my calamity and compensate me with

---

[3] Ṣaḥīḥ al-Bukhārī, Ḥadīth No. 101
[4] Sunan an-Nasā'ī, Ḥadīth No. 3429

something better than it), but Allāh will compensate him with something better than it."[5]

Allāh understands the deep pain of losing wealth or a loved one. The promise remains: with patience, we will receive something better in return. While we may not always understand why Allāh permits certain hardships, we can be assured they are ultimately for our benefit.

Sometimes, these afflictions serve as reminders or consequences of our sins. In such cases, the believer should repent and be grateful that these trials are limited to this world rather than the hereafter.

There are many perspectives to consider regarding what we label as 'bad,' as these experiences may be accompanied by hidden benefits, especially for those who are steadfast on the straight path.

The Messenger of Allāh (PBUH) said:

"How wonderful is the affair of the believer, for his affair is all good, and this applies to no one except the believer. If something good happens to him, he gives thanks and that is good for him, and if something bad happens to him, he bears it with patience, and that is good for him."[6]

With this understanding, a Muslim finds no difficulty in comprehending why 'bad things happen to good people.' They recognize the hidden good in tribulations—the idea that every cloud has a silver lining—and that these challenges may ultimately serve their best interests, especially when faced with patience and resilience.

---

[5]Sunan Ibn Majah, Hadīth No. 1598
[6]Ṣaḥīḥ Muslim, Hadīth No. 100

Given this foundation, we realize that we are not strangers to trials and tribulations, as Allāh decrees everything, both good and bad. All comes from Him.

This encapsulates the concept of *Al-Qadar*:

Allāh has predetermined all things for eternity, possessing full knowledge of what will occur at all times. He understands the specifics, the minutiae, and has willed and written them; everything unfolds according to His Perfect Decree.

From this, three key points emerge clearly: Allāh has decreed all, He knows when and how events will transpire, in what sequence they will occur, and He has written and willed it to happen. Regarding His knowledge of what will happen, He says:

"And with Him are the keys of the Ghaib (all that is hidden), none knows them but He. And He knows whatever there is in (or on) the earth and in the sea; not a leaf falls, but he knows it. There is not a grain in the darkness of the earth nor anything fresh or dry, but is written in a Clear Record." - Qur'ān, 6:59

With this understanding, the believer knows that Allāh is fully aware of everything that befalls him. This knowledge brings comfort, assuring him that he is not alone and that the oppression and misfortune he faces are not beyond Allāh's knowledge. Recognizing this, he remains patient, expecting to be rewarded for his endurance. Allāh says,

"Say: "Nothing shall ever happen to us except what Allāh has ordained for us. He is our Maulā (Lord, Helper and

Protector)." And in Allāh let the believers put their trust." - Qur'ān, 9:51

An understanding of predestination—that all is decreed—helps us feel less desperate, less anxious, and more patient, strengthening our composure to face life's challenges. Knowing that there is a divine decree, we find solace in doing our best, even if we do not fully grasp the details of Allāh's Plan, while we await His Expansive Mercy.

We engage in good deeds, assuring ourselves that we are destined for a positive outcome. This belief inspires us to act in ways that align with our ultimate success.

"Narrated by 'Alī: We were at a funeral in the graveyard of Gharqad, also called Baqī Al-Gharqad. The Prophet (PBUH) came to us, sat down, we sat around him. He had a small stick with him. Then, he leaned forward and began scraping the ground with the stick, saying, *'There is none among you, and no created soul, but has his place written for him either in Paradise or in Hell, and also has his happy or miserable fate in the Hereafter written for him.'* A man said, 'O Allāh's Messenger (PBUH)! Shall we not depend upon what has been written for us and leave the deeds?' He said, *'Perform good deeds, for everybody will find easy to do such deeds as will lead him to his destined place for which he has been created.'* Then he recited: **"As for him who gives (in charity) and keeps his duty to Allāh and believes in the best reward from Allāh...'** (Qur'ān 92:5-10)"[7]

A believer understands their lack of knowledge about the pregnant future, however, their persistence and their commitment to the straight path serves as motivation to

---

[7] Ṣaḥīḥ Al-Bukhārī, Ḥadīth No. 7551

persevere, regardless of challenges. Knowing that their worldly sustenance has been decreed, they feel content and have no desire to accumulate wealth through theft or deceit.

Consider the story of a man who was asked for help. He went to gather the needed sum—let us say USD100—but the person seeking assistance absconded with a valuable item of his. This item left a significant gap in his life, so he went to the market to find a replacement. To his surprise, he discovered his stolen item for sale, priced at USD100—the very amount he intended to give the thief. He repurchased it and remarked, *'Well, he stole what was supposed to be rightfully his; now he will have to answer to Allāh.'*

A person who believes that their share of this world, wealth, status, etc., has been justly measured will find no reason to steal. They understand they will only enjoy what is lawfully due to them by Allāh's decree if they exercise patience.

Moreover, a blessed believer in destiny is filled with gratitude, recognizing that their achievements are not solely the result of their efforts but also of Allāh's decree. They empathize with others who work hard yet face misfortune, and they express gratitude to their Lord and Creator for His blessings. When faced with denial, their belief helps them maintain composure while remaining patient, preventing feelings of regret. They do not think, *'If I had done this or that, things would be different.'*

They understand that being denied is not solely a consequence of their efforts but rather part of Allāh's decree. The Prophet (PBUH) said:

"Look at those below you and do not look at those above you, lest you belittle the favors of Allāh."[8]

And He also said,

"Be eager for what benefits you, seek help from Allāh, and do not be frustrated. If something befalls you, then do not say: If only I had done something else! Rather say: Allāh has decreed what He wills. Verily, the phrase 'if only' opens the way for the work of Satan."[9]

Belief in Destiny helps us forgive others, as we recognize that our fate—shaped by the actions of others—has been decreed. While this understanding does not absolve them of responsibility, it helps us avoid the notion that others can thwart our success. We are assured that what is meant for us will not elude us, and what is not meant for us will never reach us.

Another benefit of believing in Destiny is that it leaves no room for a superiority complex. We did not make the decisions; Allāh decreed it. Even up to your being active and another person being lazy, you as the active one, after trying to help the lazy one get better, should also remember that even being active is a gift from Allāh. Whether due to family background, culture, intelligence, or other factors, some may naturally be more goal-oriented. Instead of judging, your role is to assist those who struggle, reminding yourself of Allāh's favor in your own abilities. The Prophet (PBUH) said:

---

[8] Sunan al-Tirmidhī, No. Hadīth 2513
[9] Sunan Ibn Majah, Hadīth No. 4168

*"There is a measure for everything, even ability (resolve/vitality)
and inability (deficiency/lack of resolve)."*[10]

An-Nawawī, may Allāh have mercy upon him, commented on the Hadīth, saying, *"Ability is the opposite of inability; it is the vitality and cleverness with matters. It means that the lack of resolve of the incompetent person is predetermined, and the vitality of the capable person is predetermined..."*[11]

Al-Hāfidh Ibn Hajar, may Allāh have mercy upon him, said, *"It means that nothing takes place in the universe except with the decree, knowledge, and will of Allāh. All things are predestined and decreed by His knowledge and will. The Hadīth highlighted the person's ability and inability as such in order to indicate the fact that although our actions are known to us and intended by us, they do not come to pass except with the decree and will of Allāh..."*[12]

This serves as a reminder to the wealthy not to dismiss the poor as lazy or lacking ambition but to approach them with humility. While you may possess talent and business acumen, remember that your wealth is ultimately part of Allāh's decree.

A believer in Destiny also confronts the harsh realities of life. They understand it is possible they may never attain great riches or have children—these are genuine possibilities.

---

[10] Ṣaḥīḥ Muslim, Hadīth No. 6419

[11] An-nawawī, Sharh Ṣaḥīḥ Muslim, commentary on Hadīth No. 6419

[12] Al-Hāfidh Ibn Hajar, Fath al-Bāri, Commentary on Ṣaḥīḥ al-Bukhārī, Vol. 11, Book of Destiny (Kitāb al-Qadar), Explanation of Hadīth on the concept of predestination and human actions.

For those who fear, due to their misdeeds, that they may be destined for hellfire, this awareness prompts self-reflection and a stronger commitment to positive change. Allāh says:

"Allāh blots out what He wills and confirms (what He wills). And with Him is the Mother of the Book (Al-Lauḥ Al-Maḥfūz)"
- Qur'ān, 13:39

Ibn Abbas explains the verse, saying, *"There are two books: a book in which is erased whatever Allāh wills, and with Him is the mother of the book."*[13]

A believer in divine predestination manages fear and anxiety more effectively. They understand that the outcomes of all matters rest in Allāh's Hands. As a result, they do not fear poverty, criticism, or harm. In fact, the devil often uses the fear of poverty as a tool to mislead people.

"Shaitān (Satan) threatens you with poverty and orders you to commit Fahshā (evil deeds, illegal sexual intercourse, sins etc.); whereas Allāh promises you Forgiveness from Himself and Bounty, and Allāh is All-Sufficient for His creatures' needs, All-Knower." - Qur'ān, 2:268

In verse 267, Allāh speaks about philanthropy and the importance of giving alms in charity. He discourages the act of donating illegitimate earnings or trivial, disposable items. In this context, He emphasizes that we should give from what we truly value or love.

---

[13] Ibn Abbās, as cited in Ibn Kathīr, Tafsīr al-Qur'ān al-Azīm, on Qur'ān 13:39.

"By no means shall you attain Al-Birr (piety, righteousness, etc., it means here Allāh's Reward, i.e., Paradise), unless you spend (in Allāh's Cause) of that which you love; and whatever of good you spend, Allāh knows it well." - Qur'ān, 3:92

Allāh urges us to give from what we truly value, reminding us that the Devil threatens us with poverty to discourage our generosity. This fear may masquerade as a caution against returning to a state of need. In contrast, when the Devil intends to encourage us to do evil, he portrays our resources as abundant, tempting us to indulge recklessly.

With a belief in predestination, you can see through this deception and recognize the Devil's tactics. Remember that everything you possess comes from Allāh; He is the source of your sustenance. Ultimately, it is His pleasure you seek by giving alms from what you cherish. You may also recall the Prophet's (PBUH) statement that *'charity does not decrease wealth'*[14], motivated to give, the fear of poverty diminishes by Allāh's permission.

With a belief in Destiny, you also do not fear blame or criticism to such an extent that it makes you conceal the truth when you see a wrong clearly taking place or injustice is being done. The Prophet Muhammad (PBUH) said:

"Let not one of you belittle himself." They said, "O Messenger of Allāh, how does one belittle himself?" He said, "He finds a matter concerning Allāh about which he should speak, and he does not speak, so Allāh says to him on the Day of Resurrection: 'What prevented you from speaking concerning such-and-such?' He

---

[14] Ṣaḥīḥ Muslim, Hadīth No. 6264

says: 'The fear of people.' So Allāh says: 'Rather, it is I whom you should more rightly fear.'"[15]

And he (PBUH) also said,

"Whoever seeks Allāh's pleasure by the people's wrath, Allāh will suffice him concerning the people, and whoever seeks the people's pleasure by Allāh's wrath, Allāh will leave him to the people."[16]

Here, Allāh praises those who strive in His cause and remain unafraid of the blame from others,

"...they strive in the cause of Allāh and do not fear the blame of the blamers. That is the favor of Allāh; He bestows it upon whom He wills. And Allāh is all-Encompassing and Knowing."[17] - Qur'ān, 5:54

In this verse, we see that Allāh grants this as a favor to any of His servants whom He wills. Belief in Divine Predestination helps mitigate our fear of harm, which can otherwise prevent people from standing up for justice and being truthful, among other things. Allāh says

"It is only Shaitan (Satan) that suggests to you the fear of his Auliyā' [supporters and friends (polytheists, disbelievers in the Oneness of Allāh and in His Messenger, Muhammad)], so fear them not, but fear Me, if you are (true) believers." - Qur'ān, 3:175

And the Prophet (PBUH) said,

---

[15] Sunan Ibn Mājah, Hadīth No. 4008
[16] Sunan al-Tirmidhī¯, Hadīth No. 2414
[17] This specific translation is from Ṣaḥīḥ International

"Whoever is concerned about the Hereafter, Allāh will make him feel independent of others and will make his affairs easy for him, and the world will come to him whether he wants it or not."[18]

"Those who convey the Message of Allāh and fear Him, and fear none save Allāh. And Sufficient is Allāh as a Reckoner." - Qur'ān, 33:39

We may encounter fear of harm when our steadfast commitment to the straight path makes others feel threatened. A person who believes in predestination understands that nothing will happen except by Allāh's decree and recalls this reminder from the Prophet,

"Know that if the entire world were to gather together to benefit you with something, they would not benefit you except with what Allāh has already prescribed for you. And if they were to gather to harm you with something, they would not harm you except with what Allāh has already prescribed against you. The pens have been lifted, and the pages have dried."[19]

---

[18] Sunan Ibn Mājah, Hadīth No. 4105
[19] Sunan al-Tirmidhī, Hadīth No. 2516

12

ISLĀM; THE STRAIGHT PATH, ONLY ONE TRUE RELIGION AND COMPLETE WAY OF LIFE

IT is common to hear claims that a particular faith is *"not just **a religion**, but **a way of life.**"* Unfortunately, many of these faiths lack practical guidance on everyday matters, offering no coherent system or culture—just "God speaking" through every Tom, Dick, and Mariah.

In contrast, Islām is not merely a religion; it is a comprehensive way of thinking, speaking, and acting that shapes every aspect of life. Islām provides a moral, spiritual, and intellectual framework that guides every choice without ambiguity. It does not just claim to be a way of life—it fully demonstrates it.

One key area of confusion for many people is the role of human action in salvation—whether faith alone in the heart is sufficient. If it does, to what extent? Islām addresses these questions clearly, leaving no room for doubt. A well-versed Muslim, therefore, suffers no confusion on these matters.

Faith, Salvation, and Actions

From the proponents of *"actions speak louder than words,"* we have interestingly heard that all you need for salvation is to accept some things, and you are saved. In extreme cases, they assert that you can become infallible or above sin. And they mean it in two ways. First is the unrealistic sanctimony that you may become too righteous to sin; second is the delusion that rules may no longer apply to you. Yet, the same belief system offers quotes like *"From the abundance of the heart, the mouth speaks."* The main bone of contention here is age-long confusion about what true belief entails, and this is precisely what Allāh addresses when He says,

"O people of the Scripture (Jews and Christians): 'Why do you mix truth with falsehood and conceal the truth while you know?'" - Qur'ān, 3:71

People are not defined by what they claim to be but by who they truly are. Often, this is revealed in their actions. Proclaiming faith and belief is one thing; aligning those claims with consistent, sincere effort is another. This is why the Prophet of Islām distinguished between the actions of the people of Paradise and those of the people of Hellfire.

Islām does not dismiss the importance of faith expressed by word or held in the heart. It recognizes the value in these proclamations and internal beliefs. However, it insists that faith and good intentions must be accompanied by righteous actions. Generally, the stronger the faith, the more profound the deeds. But human judgment cannot fully grasp the true weight of good actions, as only God, the All-Knowing, can assess their sincerity.

The elephant in the room is that greater faith should naturally lead to greater good deeds, even if we cannot always measure this connection. In short, proclaiming faith is the first step toward salvation, but it must be followed by a commitment to good deeds.

Where to Start From

The journey on the Straight Path begins with accepting the truth that Islām is the correct religion and the only way to reach God Almighty. The simplest evidence for this is that Islām declares it unequivocally. As you would agree, and as we have thoroughly demonstrated, its evidence holds true.

"And whoever seeks a religion other than Islām, it will never be accepted of him, and in the Hereafter, he will be one of the losers." - Qur'ān, 3:85

This is important because no other religion makes clear, fact-based claims about being the only true path to God. Perhaps this is a mercy from Allāh and a sign meant to guide humanity. You will not find explicit scriptural statements from any other faith declaring itself as the only acceptable religion before God Almighty—such assertions are merely inferred by their followers.

Additionally, the Qur'ān stands as undeniable proof of its divine origin, being the ever-obedient word of God Almighty. As discussed earlier in this book, the evidence proves beyond doubt that Prophet Muhammad (PBUH) could not have been a false prophet (please refer to earlier chapters for more on this argument).

Furthermore, Islām is the only divinely named and clearly structured religion. As Allah clearly states:

"...Today I have perfected your faith for you, completed My favor upon you, and chosen Islam as your way..."[1] - Qur'ān, 5:3

It is also the only faith that explains the existence of other religions. Those who reject Prophet Muhammad (PBUH) while accepting Moses or Jesus as true Prophets face an inherent contradiction—they know deep down there is a problem with their claim. Islām proclaims that Moses, Jesus, and Muhammad (peace and blessings of Allāh be upon them all) were all noble messengers of the same Straight Path, that of Islām.

Anyone who denies Muhammad (PBUH) as a true Prophet will struggle to explain how Moses and Jesus, the Prophets they claim to follow, did not forewarn against someone who would "mislead" nearly 7 billion people in less than 2,000 years.[2]

---

[1] This specific translation is from Ṣaḥīḥ International
[2] Ilir, Akshija. (2018). How many Muslims have ever lived on Earth? - Reflections from demographic data of the world Muslim population.

The clarity, structure, and wisdom in Islām's guidance on life could not have been the product of an unschooled man centuries ago. This is self-evident, and accepting this undeniable truth is the first step. After acknowledging this, the next step is to reject false gods and idols.

"There is no compulsion in religion. Verily, the Right Path has become distinct from the wrong path. Whoever disbelieves in Tāghūt and believes in Allāh, then he has grasped the most trustworthy handhold that will never break. And Allāh is All-Hearer, All-Knower." - Qur'ān, 2:256

Several important points should be noted here.

First, concerning converting to Islām, the Qur'ān explicitly forbids forcing anyone to accept its spiritual authority. If this prohibition were written today, one might dismiss it as mere *"wokeness."* However, the Qur'ān was revealed in a time when it was common to impose belief systems on others, often through state-enforced religion. Yet, this verse forbade such compulsion, standing against the norms of the era.

How did an unlettered Arab, in such an environment, know what was morally right when the prevailing standard was wrong?

Second, the verse makes a bold assertion that the right path is distinct and unmistakable from any other. After reading this far, one might sincerely question whether any religion with greater clarity and comprehensiveness in its culture exists than Islām. The difference should now be evident.

Third, for anyone seeking truth and inclined toward Islām, rejecting false gods and idols is essential, dedicating one's belief to Allāh alone. For Muslims, this carries a profound lesson: it is not enough to acknowledge Allāh's sovereignty and resolve to worship Him. *Have we truly rejected 'Tāghūt' (false deities or powers)? Have we remained steadfast on the Straight Path, avoiding sinful distractions from all sides?* Every Muslim must ask themselves, *"What have I rejected as a Muslim?"*

If you cannot list a few worldly temptations that you have resisted for the sake of Islām, there may be a deeper issue. Take a moment, grab a pen and paper, and write down the things you love but have abstained from because of your commitment to the principles of Islām.

Identify those things you love that are forbidden in Islām, add them to your list, and commit to abstaining from them. And remember the words of the Prophet (PBUH),

"Indeed, you will never leave something for the sake of Allāh but that Allāh will replace it with something better."[3]

Lastly, Allāh promises a reliable, unbroken handhold to those who remain steadfast and unwavering in their commitment to the truth. In summary, the path starts with the following steps:

- **Accept the truth of Islām** *as the correct and only acceptable religion before God Almighty.*

- **Reject false gods and idols** *by ensuring nothing and no one is placed above or equal to Allāh.*

- **Follow up with good deeds** *that reflect this belief, as exemplified in the Pillars of Islām.*

---

[3] Musnad Imām Aḥmad, Hadīth No. 23074

Do Not Be a Circumstantial Muslim

"Circumstantial Muslims" are those who adopt Islām due to external influences but lack a deep understanding of its core principles. These individuals are most likely to abandon Islām, letting go of the strong handhold due to a lack of knowledge about the faith. It is often apparent in their stories.

For example, there are numerous cases of Muslims who, motivated by a distorted sense of justice against Western imperialism, join extremist groups. These groups often misuse Islām in unorthodox ways, engaging in violence against innocent civilians under a false banner of Islām. One such individual, in his misguided zeal, planned to execute a violent act but found the airport closed by Allāh's decree. Frustrated, he questioned, *"If I am fighting for Allāh, why would He allow the airport to close?"* Feeling betrayed, he left Islām.

His words reveal a profound ignorance of Islām's fundamentals—particularly the concept of Destiny (Qadar). This lack of understanding is typical among extremists, who often do not grasp even the basics of the faith. It raises the question: what exactly are they extreme about? This is why the Prophet (PBUH) said,

"Beware of going to extremes (in religion), for those before you were destroyed by going to extremes in religion."[4]

The downfall of this man, leaving Islām, stemmed from his extremism—placing his desire for fighting above the need to understand basic teachings like Divine Predes-

---

[4]Sunan al-Nasā'ī, Hadīth No. 3057

tination. He failed to grasp how Allāh decrees things we might not like for reasons we cannot comprehend.

Anyone reading this far in the book could easily explain to him that Allāh's decree is certain and supersedes his plans, expectations, environment, or true intentions. In this case, perhaps Allāh's will was to thwart his plans and prevent him from harming innocent people, offering him an opportunity to be redirected toward a better path closer to Allāh. Tragically, his ignorance blocked this chance.

This is why Islām mandates that every Muslim seek knowledge, even to the farthest places, as practicing Islām is knowledge-based, not driven by individual whims.

Seeking Knowledge Along the Way

The Prophet (PBUH) went to great lengths to teach his companions the religion, as commanded by Allāh. The companions not only listened and learned, but they also dedicated time to practicing what they learned before seeking more knowledge.

For instance, the companions might memorize and recite ten verses from the Messenger of Allāh, but they would not proceed to the next set until they fully understood the knowledge and actions contained within those verses. They would say, *"We learned sacred knowledge and action together."*[5]

This is true knowledge; unlike the fleeting flicker of a candle, it lights its surroundings yet casts a dark shadow—its own image—upon itself as it gradually fades over time. After embracing Islām, seeking knowledge becomes essen-

---

[5] Musnad Imām Aḥmad, Hadīth No. 23482

tial, as it is critical to practicing the faith completely and wholesomely. However, our motivation in seeking knowledge must not be to impress others, to recite eloquently, or to appear knowledgeable. Instead, it should be to improve ourselves and our actions first before others.

As mentioned earlier, the sincerity in seeking knowledge and aligning actions with intentions is a concept unique to Islām.

The Prophet (PBUH) spoke of the shock on the Day of Judgment when people will witness, to their horror, someone who was thought to be a wise counselor being cast into Hellfire. They will say,

"... O so-and-so! What is wrong with you? Did not you use to order us to do good deeds and forbid us to do bad deeds? He will reply: Yes, I used to order you to do good deeds, but I did not do them myself, and I used to forbid you to do bad deeds, yet I used to do them myself."[6]

Unfortunately, the pursuit of religious knowledge is not emphasized in many other faiths. First, the foundations of these religions are not broad or comprehensive enough to be a field of deep study. Second, many of these faiths do not offer their followers direct access to God, relying instead on intermediaries. Clerics often position themselves as the sole voices of God, making the personal search for divine knowledge unnecessary.

In Islām, however, it is different. An Imām or preacher only has the authority to convey what is clearly evidenced

---

[6] Ṣaḥīḥ al-Bukhārī, Hadīth No. 3267 and Ṣaḥīḥ al-Bukhārī Hadīth No. 3267

in the religion. The pursuit of knowledge is highly esteemed in Islām, as the Prophet (PBUH) said,

"Seeking knowledge is an obligation upon every Muslim."[7]

And he (PBUH) also said,

"Whoever follows a path in the pursuit of knowledge, Allāh will make a path to Paradise easy for him."[8]

As an aside, *can anyone truly believe that a deceiver—intent on misleading the masses—would encourage his followers to seek knowledge?* Deception thrives on ignorance, keeping people uneducated and unaware. Islām, in contrast, emphasizes the pursuit of knowledge. It is important to understand what you are dedicating your life to.

This emphasis on knowledge is not restricted to religious learning alone. Islām encourages Muslims to seek beneficial knowledge from all fields of human endeavor. Unsurprisingly, Muslims have made significant contributions throughout history in astronomy, mathematics, medicine, and philosophy. Excelling in these areas is seen as a way to uncover the signs of Allāh in the universe while making meaningful impacts in the lives of others and the society at large. While Islāmic knowledge takes precedence as the foundation, pursuing other beneficial knowledge is also highly valued.

We have mentioned previously how extremists, ignorant of Islām's true teachings, are manipulated to commit atrocities. There is another striking story of a brother who

---

[7]Sunan Ibn Mājah, Hadīth No. 224
[8]Sunan Ibn Mājah, Hadīth No. 225

journeyed to a different country to join a terrorist group. A week later, he was invited by the supreme leader, who glowingly gave glad tidings of a mission sanctioned for him by "Allah," but it was a suicide mission.

It is laughable how these missions are packaged to appeal to the ignorant, as anyone fully primed in the true teachings of the faith can easily see through the farce. The leader literally asked if he would want to dine with the Prophet in paradise that very day. He was expected to be ecstatic at the opportunity of being elected by Allah to carry out this 'sacred' service of killing innocent men, women, children, and himself in the process. The brother, at that juncture, had realized how disingenuous, how cunning the whole setup. He was intrepid enough to hazard a quick succession of questions to the leader:

"How long again did you say you and your group have been fighting this war?" The leader replied, *"before the time of Osāma Bin Laden."* Then came the follow-up question: *"How come, with all your long years of dedicated devotion, Allāh never saw it fitting to choose you—our leader—to dine with His prophet in paradise? Why would he keep skipping you the entire time to choose me, who has only been here a little over a week?"*

In this way, we should be prepared to question those who misuse faith for their immoral purposes.

Living a Life of Submission

After accepting the truth, learning about it, and implementing it, the next step is to persist in living under the guidance of Islām. Such a person never considers themselves wiser than their Creator, who established the laws of Islām. They recognize that they were created solely to worship Allāh, as He says,

"And I (Allāh) created not the jinns and humans except they should worship Me (Alone)." - Qur'ān 51:56

This connection is the most powerful and effective way to reform a person. It succeeds where force fails.

In the United States, the Eighteenth Amendment outlawed the manufacture, transportation, and sale of alcohol nationwide, beginning in 1920. This era of Prohibition lasted 13 years, until 1933. The result? Millions of Americans resorted to consuming alcohol illegally, leading to widespread illicit production and sale and inadvertently fueling the rise of organized crime. In short, the effort failed spectacularly, even contributing to an increase in crime, ultimately leading to the repeal of the law. It begs the question: *how did a country that once banned alcohol become one of the world's largest manufacturers?*

In contrast, during the lifetime of Prophet Muhammad (PBUH), the prohibition of alcohol was revealed as a divine command from Allāh through the Prophet.

"O you who believe! Intoxicants (all kinds of alcoholic drinks), gambling, Al-Ansāb , and al-Azlām (arrows for seeking luck or decision) are an abomination of Shaitān's (Satan) handiwork. So avoid (strictly all) that (abomination) in order that you may be successful." - Qur'ān, 5:90

Some companions recorded that soon after the verse prohibiting alcohol was revealed, those who held cups of alcohol immediately dropped them. Some, who had taken a sip, spat it out. Others, who had already consumed it, tried to induce vomiting. The streets of Madinah were flooded with discarded alcohol.[9]

No one was arrested, threatened, or killed. This reflects the binding power of true understanding—truly knowing God, the Creator of all, and the necessity of obeying Him without hesitation. In that understanding, we find contentment, knowing that whatever He commands is for our own good, whether or not it aligns with our personal desires.

Some might ask, *"Is this not a form of mind control?"* The critical question is: **who is the controller?** The Prophet (PBUH) provided a standing instruction: to learn, making the pursuit of knowledge obligatory for everyone, Muslim or not. Islām, free from new revelations and intermediaries, inherently prevents mind control. It is far easier to manipulate the ignorant but not the seeker of knowledge, as Islām exhorts.

In contrast, Islām offers a clear way out of the endless confusion and mind games that this life can present. The clarity comes when we find the Straight Path within our hearts and hold firmly to its guidance.

This is evident in 'Āishah's account of the earliest Qur'ānic revelations. She noted that the first verses revealed were healing for the hearts of the new converts, connecting them to Allāh and preparing them to accept later the verses filled with commands on what is lawful and unlawful. Their hearts were softened and ready to receive the new instructions after being nurtured by the earlier healing verses. She emphasized that had the process been reversed, it

---

[9] Ṣaḥīḥ al-Bukhārī Ḥadīth No.4620

would have been disastrous.[10]

Once a Muslim's heart is inclined toward pleasing Allāh alone, a desire to serve Him grows. This service, in turn, increases their spirituality and understanding, which naturally permeates into their daily actions.

The Five Pillars of Islām

In line with the verbal proclamation of faith, we must perform certain obligatory actions that demonstrate our unwavering loyalty to Allāh. These actions benefit the believer as they continue steadfastly on the Straight Path. These five essential practices, collectively known as the Pillars of Islām, are foundational to a Muslim's life. The first of these pillars, which forms the core of this book, focuses on faith, while the others are practical acts of worship.

1. Ash-Shahādah (The Testimony of Faith)

The testimony of faith, the Shahādah, is the foundation of Islām, declaring, *"There is no god but Allāh, and Muhammad is His messenger."* This declaration signifies complete submission to Allāh's sovereignty and will. Over a thousand years before modern psychology began discussing the power of affirmations, Islām had already emphasized the importance of verbal declaration. Today, studies show that verbal affirmations reduce stress, boost confidence, increase resilience, and improve overall well-being. In Islām, these benefits are woven into the daily repetition of the Shahādah, which continually redirects a Muslim's focus onto the Straight Path, serving as the

---

[10]Ṣaḥīḥ al-Bukhārī, Hadīth No. 4993

greatest of all supplications.

The Prophet (PBUH) taught the immense power of the Shahādah through the story of Prophet Musa (PBUH), who asked Allāh for a unique supplication. Allāh instructed him to say, *"There is no god but Allāh."* When Musa expressed surprise, noting that everyone already says this, Allāh replied, *"If all of creation were placed on one side of a scale and this statement of Tawhīd on the other, it would outweigh everything."*[11]

The Kalimat ash-Shahādah is the declaration that brings one into the fold of Islām. It consists of two parts: first, the affirmation of Allāh's oneness (Tawhīd), and second, belief in Muhammad (PBUH) as His final Prophet and Messenger. This second part, known as Kalimat al-Ittibā', emphasizes the importance of following the Prophet's guidance. Proclaiming the Shahādah with firm conviction makes one a Muslim, solidifying faith in both Allāh and His Messenger.

2. As-Salāt (Prayer)

This special act of prayer, as-Salāt, is the most important form of worship in Islām. Performed five times a day, it serves as a constant reminder of our duties to Allāh, maintaining our spiritual connection and providing a firm handhold to the Creator. While a Muslim may pray at any time, the five daily prayers are unique—structured and set at specific times for every Muslim.

The benefits of as-Salāt are abundant. It provides regular moments of redirection, allowing us to step away from the daily grind to remember and reconnect with the Creator, the very reason for our existence. Its meditative na-

---

[11]Annasā'ī from Al-Sunan Al-kubrā 10670, Ibn Hibbān, 6218

ture enhances mindfulness and presence, while the discipline of scheduled prayers improves time management and fosters a sense of responsibility. As-Salāt also offers the comfort of knowing that we are in constant communication with the All-Powerful Source of our existence.

In addition, as-Salāt fosters a deep sense of unity and brotherhood. Over a billion Muslims from all races and tribes perform the same prayer, in the same manner, at the same times, standing shoulder to shoulder, toe to toe, forming one unified body of believers. Through these organized prayers, Islām defeats racism effortlessly.

Allāh says,

"O mankind! We have created you from a male and a female, and made you into nations and tribes, that you may know one another. Verily, the most honorable of you with Allāh is that (believer) who has At-Taqwā [i.e., one of the Muttaqūn (pious]. Verily, Allāh is All-Knowing, All-Aware." – Qur'ān, 49:13

Congregational prayer is held at designated times throughout the day, always initiated by the Adhān—the call to prayer. The person chosen to sound this call in a community is called the Mu'adhin. Remarkably, the very first Mu'adhin in Islām was a black man in an Arab society, a former slave freed by a Muslim from the cruel hands of his aristocratic Arab owners. This inclusion, often idealized and misused today, has been a foundational principle of Islām from its inception.

3. Zakāt (Mandatory Charity)

Zakāt is a mandatory form of almsgiving designed to support those in need and ensure the fair redistribution of wealth from the affluent to the less fortunate. It helps to purify wealth. Unlike voluntary charity, Zakāt is obligatory and governed by specific guidelines for both its collection and equitable distribution.

Under this system, the wealthy are required to give 2.5 percent of their unused wealth—idle for a year—to the poor. The minimum threshold for Zakāt payment is set above the earnings of an average person, exempting them from this obligation. This stands in contrast to other faiths, where everyone, regardless of their financial status, must pay a significant percentage of their income.

Additionally, Islām does not leave the distribution of Zakāt to the whims of individuals, preventing leaders from abusing it or turning it into a system of favoritism. It goes directly from the rich to the poor and not from the rich to even wealthier religious leaders. The designated recipients of Zakāt are clearly defined: the poor, the needy, stranded travelers, those burdened by debt, paying for the freedom of slaves, those working in the cause of Allāh, new converts to Islām, and those responsible for distributing the Zakāt.

4. As-Sawm (Fasting)

Fasting during the sacred month of Ramadan serves as a means of spiritual purification and self-discipline. It fosters empathy for the less privileged and deepens our connection with Allāh.

Interestingly, modern scientific research also supports the benefits of intermittent fasting, highlighting its positive effects on gut health, weight management, and the prevention of various chronic diseases.

Fasting during Ramadan unites Muslims worldwide,

breaking down tribal and racial barriers since the same guidelines apply to everyone. It also encourages good neighborliness, as communities gather to share food at dusk when the fast is broken.

This is a powerful example of how Islām encourages positive behavior. As the Prophet (PBUH) said,

"Whoever gives food for a fasting person to break his fast, he will have a reward like theirs, without that detracting from their reward in the slightest."[12]

Through practices like these, the wealthy let their guard down during Ramadan (an act they are encouraged to uphold even outside of Ramadan), mingling freely with the less privileged at public Iftār dinners. They often invite the poor into their homes, seeking the rewards of charity and generosity from God.

Ramadan becomes a communal experience, fostering a healthy competition toward righteousness—one that transcends borders and includes all, creating a global, inclusive community.

5. Hajj (Pilgrimage)

Hajj is the pilgrimage to the sacred sites in Makkah and Madīnah—a once-in-a-lifetime obligation for those who are physically and financially able. It represents a journey of spiritual renewal and stands as a powerful symbol of Islāmic unity.

One of the profound aspects of Hajj is the opportunity for Muslims to physically and mentally be present at the

---

[12] Sunan Ibn Mājah, Hadīth No. 1746

ISLĀM; THE STRAIGHT PATH, ONLY ONE TRUE RELIGION AND COMPLETE WAY OF LIFE

very locations where pivotal moments in history unfolded, shaping the course of the world. Islām places great emphasis on being realistic, so much so that a Prophet of Allāh once asked Him, *"My Lord! Show me how You give life to the dead."*[13]

His question was neither out of line nor born from any sense of doubt. Rather, as recorded in Islām, it was a sincere and earnest desire for information to strengthen our faith. And yes, Islām is that realistic.

In the same spirit, the Prophet (PBUH) taught us prayers to recite when troubled by doubt. He could have simply insisted that the truth of the religion leaves no room for uncertainty. While we are indeed called to believe with certainty, Islām still offers a prayer to guard against doubt, acknowledging human nature.

In the same token, visiting the places of historical significance during Hajj strengthens faith. Hajj unites Muslims of all races and backgrounds, all dressed in the same simple white garment. It humbles the rich and powerful, uplifts the poor and downtrodden, and reminds everyone that beyond social ranks and titles, we are all mortals, destined to return to Allāh with nothing but our deeds.

Ultimate Success

A Muslim understands that this world is merely a passage to the hereafter. Those whose evil deeds outweigh their good will be cast into the Hellfire, while those whose good deeds outweigh their evil will achieve ultimate success and be welcomed into Paradise, where they will dwell

---

[13] Qur'ān, 2:260

forever.

In Paradise, there will be no death, no sickness, and no fatigue—a place created for eternal joy and unceasing pleasure, something beyond any human comprehension.

"Say: (O Muhammad) "Is that (torment) better or the Paradise of Eternity promised to the Muttaqūn (pious and righteous persons)?" It will be theirs as a reward and as a final destination. For them there will be therein all that they desire, and they will abide (there forever). It is a promise binding upon your Lord that must be fulfilled." - Qur'ān, 25:15-16

Paradise is reserved for believers—those who have surrendered their will to God and faithfully followed the teachings of the many Prophets of God, even before the arrival of the final Prophet, Muhammad (PBUH). Thus, the term Muslim, meaning a submitter to God, encompasses not only those who identify as Muslims but also those who accept Islām before their death, regardless of their prior beliefs.

However, not all who bear Muslim names or claim to be Muslims are true in their faith. Many lack a proper understanding of the religion's fundamentals and, in their ignorance, may engage in actions or beliefs that nullify their Islām.

For example, some Muslims seek spiritual help from sources other than Allāh, wear talismans, or practice black magic. Others, due to cultural influences, may pray through saints or intermediaries. These actions, along with others, can invalidate one's Islām, as the faith is based on true knowledge and the rejection of associating partners with Allāh.

A Muslim must grasp the basics, which are not complicated, and avoid anything that involves shirk (associating partners with Allāh). A person who dies in this state of shirk without sincere repentance will not be forgiven, as this is the only unforgivable sin after death. Allāh says,

"Verily, Allāh forgives not that partners should be set up with him in worship, but He forgives except that (anything else) to whom He pleases, and whoever sets up partners with Allāh in worship, he has indeed invented a tremendous sin." - Qur'ān, 4:48

A sinful Muslim who fails to repent in this life and is not forgiven may be cleansed of their sins in Hellfire for a designated period before ultimately being admitted into Paradise.

The Prophet (PBUH) said about this:

"Do you know who the muflis (bankrupt one) is? The muflis from my Ummah is one who comes on the Day of Judgment having performed prayer, fasting, and giving zakāt. However, along with all of this, he abused this person and slandered that person, ate the wealth of this person, and unlawfully spilled the blood of that person. These people will take from his good deeds. If, however, his good deeds become exhausted, then their sins will be put upon him, and he will be thrown into the Fire."[14]

From the above, we learn that we must be especially cautious about how we treat others. If we reflect, we see that many of our problems on the Day of Judgment arise from our wrongdoings in violating the rights of others.

---

[14] Ṣaḥīḥ Muslim, Hadīth No. 2581

Therefore, in the next chapter, we will discuss how to cultivate a strong Muslim character and how one should interact with others.

13

THE MUSLIM PERSONALITY AND CONDUCT

JUST as Islām goes beyond the heart—requiring both the verbal proclamation of faith and corresponding actions—it also extends beyond acts of worship focused solely on personal growth.

Our beliefs, words, and actions must bear fruits that benefit others. If they do not, it is essential to reflect on our belief system and the practices that accompany it.

Your Islām, as a Muslim, must positively impact others. Allāh says,

"And We have sent you (O Muhammad) not but as a mercy for the 'Ālamīn (mankind, jinns and all that exists)." - Qur'ān, 21:107

And the Prophet (PBUH) handed this task to us, saying,

"The believer is friendly and befriended, for there is no goodness in one who is neither friendly nor befriended. The best of people are those who are most beneficial to people."[1]

Here, we learn that we must be a source of mercy and compassion to others, treating people with kindness and friendliness. The best among us are those who benefit others the most.

That said, we know that dealing with people can be challenging. At times, you may feel the urge to withdraw into seclusion to avoid conflict. Yet, the Prophet (PBUH), acknowledging these feelings, encouraged us by saying,

"The believer who mixes with people and bears any annoyance they cause with patience is better than the believer who does not mix with people and does not bear any annoyance they cause with patience."[2]

The emphasis on tolerating and coexisting with others, showing patience and understanding for their mistakes, is so significant that it could warrant an entirely separate discussion.

One common area of conflict among people is in business dealings, particularly concerning money and debt. On this matter, the Prophet (PBUH) advised,

"May Allāh have mercy on a man who is tolerant when selling, buying, and seeking repayment."[3]

---

[1] al-Muʿjam al-Awsaṭ lil-Ṭabarāʾnī, 5937
[2] Sunan Ibn Mājah, Hadīth No. 4032
[3] Sunan Ibn Mājah, Hadīth No. 2203

In another instance, he (PBUH) says,

"Allāh the Exalted will admit a man into Paradise who was easy in his buying and selling, in his paying debts and seeking repayments."[4]

At this point, it is easy to envision how someone who faithfully adheres to Islāmic teachings would treat others. In many instances, such a person prioritizes doing good for others and easing their burdens above his own personal interests. Again, the Prophet says,

"The angels received the soul of a man who lived before you. They said: 'Have you done anything good?' The man said no. They said: 'Try to remember.' The man said: 'I used to give loans and I would order my servants to be lenient with those in difficulty and to give relief even to those who could repay.' Allāh the Exalted said: 'Thus, you will be relieved.'"

Given the emphasis on peaceful coexistence and patience with others, *what is the place of violent redress in Islām?*

First, the few verses in the Qur'ān that permit fighting are exactly what they are—permissions. This means that the default in Islām is peace. However, in situations where peace can only be achieved through armed struggle, Islām permits fighting, but with clear, unequivocal conditions outlined as follows:

"Permission to fight is given to those (i.e. believers against disbelievers), who are fighting them, (and) because they (believers) have been wronged, and surely, Allāh is Able to give them (believers) victory" - Qur'ān, 22:39

---

[4]Sunan An-Nasā'ī, Hadīth No. 4696

If fighting non-believers were the norm, the verse would not explicitly refer to it as **permission**—it would be a standard command. Importantly, the verse clearly specifies who may fight: **"those who are fought."** It also provides a crucial reason: **"for they have been wronged."** Consider that this was revealed in a society where fighting for supremacy and territorial expansion was commonplace, yet here, fighting is framed as **a permission, not a command**. It defines who is allowed to fight and under what conditions: when they (or other innocents) have been wronged. This highlights the fundamentally peaceful nature of Islām.

Moreover, the Qur'ān imposes even stricter restrictions on fighting, stating,

"Allāh does not forbid you to deal justly and kindly with those who fought not against you on account of religion and did not drive you out of your homes. Verily, Allāh loves those who deal with equity. It is only as regards those who fought against you on account of religion, and have driven you out of your homes, and helped to drive you out, that Allāh forbids you to befriend them. And whosoever will befriend them, then such are the Zālimūn (wrong-doers those who disobey Allāh)." - Qur'ān, 60:8-9

there are even other detailed conditions involved, like criteria of who can participate in it and how not to involve the lives of children and women, etc., that we may not be able to discuss here. Islam even prohibits cutting off trees during battle or war, a sign of preserving nature and protecting the climate as a priority over defeating an enemy.

The main idea here is that the foundation of a Muslim's relationships is rooted in goodness. When a Muslim speaks, the Prophet (PBUH) said,

"Say what is good or remain silent."[5]

In the more comprehensive version of this narration, the Prophet (PBUH) connects even more actions to the core of our beliefs. He (PBUH) says,

"He who believes in Allāh and the Last Day should speak good or keep silent, and he who believes in Allāh and the Last Day should be generous to his guest, and he who believes in Allāh and the Last Day should honor his neighbor."[6]

These are some of the acts of kindness a Muslim must extend to others, regardless of their faith. The Qur'an also teaches us that Allāh specifically loves those who do good.

"...truly, Allāh loves Al-Muḥsinūn (the good-doers)." - Qur'ān, 2:195

Even for treacherous people cursed by Allāh, He instructs us to forgive them while making exceptions for specific individuals in His criticism.

"So because of their breach of their covenant, We cursed them, and made their hearts grow hard. They change the words from their (right) places and have abandoned a good part of the Message that was sent to them. And you will not cease to

---

[5] Ṣaḥīḥ al-Bukhārī, Hadīth No. 6136
[6] Ṣaḥīḥ al-Bukhārī, Hadīth No. 6018

*discover deceit in them, except a few of them. But forgive them,
and overlook (their misdeeds). Verily, Allāh loves
Al-Muḥsinūn (good-doers)"* - Qur'ān, 5:13

A Muslim is encouraged to view every moment as an opportunity to do good, seeing every part of his body as a tool for acts of kindness. The Prophet (PBUH) beautifully expressed this when he said,

"On every person's joints or small bones (i.e. fingers and toes), there is sadaqah (charity) every day the sun rises. Doing justice between two people is sadaqah; assisting a man to mount his animal or lifting up his belongings onto it is sadaqah; a good word is sadaqah; every step you take towards prayer is sadaqah; and removing harmful things from pathways is sadaqah."[7]

Even for those the Prophet (PBUH) knew were not Muslims and did not meet a favorable end, he still honored their corpses after their death, as it is narrated,

"A funeral procession passed in front of the Prophet, and he stood up. When he was told that it was the coffin of a Jew, he said, "Was it not a living being (soul)?"[8]

We do not need to know someone personally to extend kindness to them. The Prophet (PBUH) said,

"Removing harmful things from the road is an act of charity (sadaqah)."[9]

---

[7] Ṣaḥīḥ al-Bukhārī, Hadīth No. 2989
[8] Ṣaḥīḥ al-Bukhārī, Hadīth No. 399
[9] Ṣaḥīḥ Muslim, Hadīth No. 2618

Continuing to safeguard the interests of others, He (PBUH) said,

"Beware of the three acts that cause you to be cursed: relieving yourselves in shaded places (that people utilize), in a walkway, or a watering place."[10]

Good Character as Proof of Faith

The Prophet (PBUH) made a statement that implied he had one singular mission. He (PBUH) said,

"I have been sent to perfect good character."[11]

The scholars of Islām explained that good character is the strongest proof of the faith with which one is raised. In other words, a Muslim with good character is a living testament to their faith. This should be a concern for any Muslim known for bad behavior or a poor reputation. The Prophet (PBUH) further connected this to the love of Allāh when he said,

"The most beloved of you to Allāh is the best of you in character"[12]

He connected good character to the scale that measures one's good and bad deeds when he (PBUH) said,

"There is nothing weightier in the scales than good morals and manners."[13]

---

[10] Sunan Abī Dāwūd, Hadīth No. 26

[11] Imām Mālik al-Muwaṭṭa, Hadīth No. 1614, Al-adab al-Mufrad Book 14, Hadīth No. 273

[12] Sunan al-Tirmidhī, Hadīth No. 2018

[13] Sunan al-Tirmidhī, Hadīth No. 2003

He equated good character with key acts of worship, as demonstrated in various instances. He (PBUH) said,

"Truly, the believer can reach, by means of good manners and morals, the degree of one who constantly fasts."[14]

And he refers to it as the completion of faith when he (PBUH) said,

"Verily, the believers with the most complete faith are those with the most excellent character and who are most kind to their families."[15]

The Prophet (PBUH) also said,

"The most complete of the believers in faith are those with the most excellent character, and the best of you are the best in behavior to their women."[16]

The Beautiful Struggle: Expect Imperfections

A Muslim will not always meet the ideal standards of Islāmic virtue in every situation, every day. Such perfection belongs to Allāh alone. However, a Muslim must strive, in every possible way, to reach the highest standards of virtue in both words and actions. This is what personal development looks like in Islām—the ongoing effort to improve oneself daily.

It is a continuous struggle to be better, motivated by Allāh's forgiveness when one falters and by His love for

---

[14] Sunan Abī Dāwūd, Hadīth No. 4798
[15] Sunan al-Tirmidhī, Hadīth No. 2612
[16] Sunan al-Tirmidhī, Hadīth No. 1162

those who do good. The Muslim understands that this journey is unceasing but also knows he is rewarded for his efforts. Thus, he does not despair, finding peace between the fear of Allāh and hope in His mercy.

"Verily, We have created man in toil." - Qur'ān, 90:4

It is essential for everyone to have this simple understanding: by doing so, we can pardon and excuse one another. Yes, this individual is a Muslim, and yes, Islām teaches these virtues, but they are also human—fallible and always capable of striving for better. Our role is to support their improvement, not to tarnish their honor by tearing them down. This is where the importance of calling one another to patience and truth comes into play.

"By Al-'Asr (the time). Verily! Man is in loss, except those who believe (in Islāmic Monotheism) and do righteous good deeds, and recommend one another to the truth, and recommend one another to patience." - Qur'ān, 103:1-3

Goodness to Self and Family

Islām also encourages us to turn that kindness inward toward ourselves. However, let us first consider our closest unit—our families. Kindness to parents is so vital that Allāh mentions it immediately after forbidding the association of partners with Him. He says,

"And your Lord has decreed that you worship none but Him. And that you be dutiful to your parents. If one of them or both of them attain old age in your life, say not to them a word of

disrespect, nor shout at them but address them in terms of honor. And lower unto them the wing of submission and humility through mercy, and say: "My Lord! Bestow on them Your Mercy as they did bring me up when I was small." - Qur'ān, 17:23-24

The Prophet (PBUH) emphasized this further when he informed us, saying,

"The pleasure of the Lord is in the pleasure of the parents, and the displeasure of the Lord is in the displeasure of the parents."[17]

The only time we are not expected to obey or honor our parents is when they ask us to do things that contradict Allah's legislation.

Islām further prohibits cutting off communication with our siblings or close relatives and encourages maintaining ties of kinship, even if they are non-Muslims.

"He who believes in Allāh and the Last Day, let him maintain good relations with kins."[18]

If such relatives sever the bond, we are still encouraged to reconnect and maintain the relationship; as the Prophet (PBUH) said,

"The one who maintains good relations with his relatives, even if they sever ties with him, is the one who truly upholds the ties of kinship."[19]

---

[17] Sunan al-Tirmidhī, Hadīth No. 1899
[18] Ṣaḥīḥ al-Bukhārī, Hadīth No. 6138
[19] Ṣaḥīḥ al-Bukhārī, Hadīth No. 5988

This aligns with the general principle of repaying bad with good. Allāh says,

"The good deed and the evil deed cannot be equal. Repel (the evil) with one which is better, then verily! he, between whom and you there was enmity, (will become) as though he was a close friend." - Qur'ān, 41:34

Turning to the self, the Prophet (PBUH) advised against overburdening ourselves with excessive religious acts.

"Religion is easy, and no one overburdens himself in his religion, but he will be unable to continue in that way. So do not be extremists but try to be near perfection and receive the good tidings that you will be rewarded. Gain strength by worshiping in the mornings and afternoons and during the last hours of the night."[20]

He addressed gut health centuries before scientists began to understand its importance when he (PBUH) said:

"Man does not fill a container more evil than his belly. It is sufficient for a man to eat that amount which straightens his back [i.e., a few morsels to gain some energy]. If this is not possible, then a third for food, a third for drink, and a third for air."[21]

Unlike those who created their own religions, the Prophet of Islām had no ego to defend. He emphasized the power of spoken prayers while also instructing that medicine should not be disregarded. He (PBUH) said,

---

[20] Ṣaḥīḥ al-Bukhāri, Hadīth No. 39
[21] Sunan Tirmidhī, Hadīth No. 2380 and Sunan Ibn Mājah, Hadīth No. 3349

"Make use of medical treatment, for Allāh has not made a disease without appointing a remedy for it, with the exception of old age."[22]

When he was informed of the overzealous claims of some of his companions, who vowed to worship continuously without rest or sleep, he corrected them. He (PBUH) said regarding rest,

"Your body has a right over you, your eyes have a right over you, and your wife has a right over you."[23]

The Prophet (PBUH) also emphasized the importance of personal hygiene, which was not as common in his time as it is today. Over 1,400 years ago, he made Friday baths obligatory for his followers—a practice that might seem ordinary now but was groundbreaking back then. He (PBUH) said,

"Five practices are of the fitrah (natural disposition): circumcision, shaving the pubic region, clipping the nails, and cutting the mustaches short."[24]

Kindness in Islām is all-encompassing, and any researcher would be struck by the high value the Prophet Muhammad (PBUH) placed on kindness to animals. This was at a time when animals were often seen as nothing more than sources of food, labor, or targets for sport. He said,

---

[22] Sunan Abī Dāwūd, Hadīth No. 3855
[23] Ṣaḥīḥ al-Bukhārī, Hadīth 127
[24] Ṣaḥīḥ al-Bukhārī, Hadīth No. 779

"Fear Allāh in your treatment of animals."[25]

He (PBUH) also forbade killing animals for sport, saying,

"If someone kills a sparrow for fun, the sparrow will cry out on the Day of Judgment, 'O Lord! That person killed me in vain! He did not kill me for any useful purpose.'"[26]

In a touching instance, when some of his companions took two chicks (or eggs) from their mother, he instructed them to return them, as the mother was distressed.[27] For animals slaughtered for food, he emphasized that it should be done in the most humane and least stressful way.[28] He said,

"Allāh has ordained kindness (and excellence) in everything. If the killing (of animals) is to be done, do it in the best manner, and when you slaughter, do it in the best manner, sharpen the knife, and put the animal at ease."[29]

Finally the Noble Prophet Muhammad (PBUH) makes us understand that kindness to animals can attract Allah's forgiveness for our misgivings and sins. He said,

"A prostitute was forgiven by Allah, because, passing by a panting dog near a well and seeing that the dog was about to die of thirst,

---

[25] Sunan Abī Dāwūd, Hadīth No. 2548

[26] Sunan An-Nasā'ī, Hadīth No. 4446

[27] Al-Adab Al-Mufrad No. 382

[28] This is one of the requirements for what Muslims refer to *Halāl* food when it comes to the meat that is considered pure to eat.

[29] Ṣaḥīḥ Muslim, Hadīth No. 1955

she took off her shoe, and tying it with her head-cover she drew out some water for it. So, Allah forgave her because of that."[30]

---

[30] Ṣaḥīḥ al-Bukhārī, Ḥadīth No. 3321

14

THE CALL TO THE STRAIGHT PATH

As we began, the first thing we pose to Allāh in our prayers is guidance to the Straight Path. Walking this path removes life's confusions, brings clarity and certainty, and makes us mindful of Allāh by recognizing His signs and striving for goodness through conscious action. It keeps us relying on Allāh, who offers the strongest support against life's many challenges. This reliance stems from a deeper understanding of trials. The Straight Path is the surest route to true tranquility, as discussed in the previous chapters. It enables us to be at our best during times of hardship and ease alike.

The Straight Path is Islām itself, and even as Muslims, we must continuously seek Allāh's guidance to stay on course, as many distractions could lead us astray.

Whoever does not safeguard their faith does not truly value it. Whoever does not cherish Islām does not truly understand it. And that alone is reason enough to hold it dear.

Commenting on the verse,

"And verily, this (i.e., Allāh's Commandments mentioned in the prior two Verses 151 and 152) is my Straight Path, so follow it, and follow not (other) paths, for they will separate you away from His Path. This He has ordained for you that you may become Al-Muttaqūn (the pious)." - Qur'ān, 6:153

Ibn Jarīr recorded that a man once asked Ibn Mas'ūd, "What is the straight path?" He replied, "Muhammad (PBUH) left us at its lower end, and its other end is in paradise. To the right of this path are other paths, and to the left of it are other parts, and there are men "on these paths" calling those who pass them. Whoever goes on the other paths will end up in the hellfire. Whoever takes the Straight Path will end up in Paradise"

The Prophet Muhammad (PBUH) said about this,

"Allāh has given a parable of the straight path, and on the two sides of this path, there are two walls containing doorways. On these doorways, there are curtains that are lowered down. On the gate of this path, there is a caller heralding, 'O people! come and enter the straight path altogether, and do not divide.' There is also another caller that heralds from above the path, who says when a person wants to remove the curtain on any of these doors, 'Woe to you! Do not open this door, for if you open it, you will enter it. The (straight) path is Islām, the two walls are Allāh's set limits,

the open doors lead to Allāh's prohibitions, the caller on the gate of the path is Allāh's Book (the Qur'ān), while the caller from above the path is Allāh's admonition in the heart of every Muslim."[1]

Being on the Straight Path is more about disavowing sins and striving to bow to Allāh's Will, all to the best of our ability and for the ultimate betterment of ourselves.

We can handpick a few points from the Hadīth sourced from Tafsir Ibn Kathir.

The first point is that the distractions from the Straight Path come with their own callers or detractors. These callers invite towards evil, while Allāh calls towards goodness. Allāh says,

"So (O Muhammad) obey not the deniers [(of Islāmic Monotheism those who belie the Verses of Allāh), the Oneness of Allāh, and the Messenger of Allāh (Muhammad), etc.] They wish that you should compromise (in religion out of courtesy) with them, so they (too) would compromise with you. And obey not everyone who swears much, and is considered worthless." - Qur'ān 68:8-10

Those on the Straight Path must recognize the callers to evil and distance themselves, lest they be lured into wrongdoing.

The second point is that we can open the door to sin by merely pulling back the curtain. A person who approaches fornication, for example, is pulling back that curtain, and as the warner cautioned, once it is opened, it can lead to self-destruction and falling off the path.

---

[1] Sunan al-Tirmidhī, Hadīth No. 2859

The guidance here is clear: *we must avoid even approaching sinful actions, not just the sinful actions themselves.*

"And come not near to the unlawful sexual intercourse. Verily, it is a Fāhishah [i.e. anything that transgresses its limits (a great sin)], and an evil way." - Qur'ān, 17:32

Here, we find the principle of avoiding close proximity to sin and rejecting the influence of those who promote it. Unfortunately, even among believers today, we may develop affinities with individuals who do not reflect our values—such as celebrities who openly promote societal immorality.

"Verily, those who like that (the crime of) illegal sexual intercourse should be propagated among those who believe, they will have a painful torment in this world and in the Hereafter. And Allāh knows and you know not." - Qur'ān, 24:19

We must recognize these callers to evil and try to avoid them and their influence, especially if we are to remain on the Straight Path.

The key point is that we must not approach or test the limits set by Allāh. We should not feel comfortable simply because we have not crossed those boundaries yet. Being too close to the edge is almost like crossing it.

"...These are the limits (set) by Allāh, so approach them not. Thus does Allāh make clear His Āyāt (proofs, evidences, lessons, signs, revelations, verses, laws, legal and illegal things, Allāh's set limits, orders, etc.) to mankind that they may become Al-Muttaqūn (the pious)." - Qur'ān, 2:187

We must approach these limits with Taqwa, often translated as one's consciousness of Allāh. A particular narration that illustrates the essence of Taqwā also provides guidance on how to navigate these boundaries.

Umar ibn Khattab (RA) once asked Ubay Ibn Ka'ab (RA) the definition of Taqwa. In reply, Ibn Ka'ab asked, *"Have you ever had to traverse a thorny path?"* Umar replied in the affirmative; Ubay Bin Ka'ab continued, *"How do you do so?"* Umar said he would carefully walk through, having first collected together the loose endings of flowy clothing in his hands so nothing is snagged or caught by the thorns abrading his skin by extension. Ka'ab said, *"This is the definition of taqwā, to protect oneself from sin through life's dangerous journey so that one might successfully complete the journey unscathed by sin."*[2]

A Muslim does not rush into anything without first understanding the Islāmic ruling on the matter (to find guidance on religious-related matters specifically). He is cautious and deliberate. He does not think, *"Since this is permitted, I can do it however I please."* Instead, he exercises moderation in his actions and is especially careful not to cross the boundaries Allāh sets. All the while, he ensures his actions align with the way and method of the Prophet (PBUH). He does not recklessly sit on the borderline, casually saying, *"It is not that Harām!"* Rather, he avoids doubtful matters out of caution. The Prophet (PBUH) said,

"That which is lawful (halāl) is clear, and that which is unlawful (harām) is clear, and between the two of them are doubtful matters about which not many people know. Thus, he who avoids

---

[2]Tafsīr ibn Kathīr, Surah Al-Baqarah, Verse: 2, vol. 1, pg. 255

doubtful matters clears himself in regard to his religion and his honor, but he who falls into doubtful matters falls into that which is unlawful, like the shepherd who pastures around a sanctuary, all but grazing therein. Truly every king has a sanctuary, and truly Allāh's sanctuary is His prohibitions..."[3]

The fourth benefit of the Hadīth is the presence of two callers: one is the Qur'ān, and the other is Allāh's constant guidance through the heart's natural inclination to Islām, tugging at the heart of every Muslim in admonition. Regarding the Qur'ān, Allāh says,

"(He has made it) Straight to give warning (to the disbelievers) of a severe punishment from Him, and to give glad tidings to the believers (in the Oneness of Allāh Islāmic Monotheism), who work righteous deeds, that they shall have a fair reward (i.e. Paradise)." - Qur'ān, 18:2

And He also said,

"It (this Qur'ān) is only a Reminder for all the 'Ālamīn (mankind and jinns)." - Qur'ān, 38:87

Now, consider the mindset of someone who claims to believe but pays little attention to the Qur'ān. Where do they expect to find guidance to avoid prohibited actions? Where will they take their cues from? The Prophet (PBUH) also emphasized the link between our relationship with the Qur'ān and our ultimate success or failure. He (PBUH) said,

---

[3] Ṣaḥīḥ al-Bukhārī, Hadīth No. 52, Ṣaḥīḥ Muslim, Hadīth No. 1599

"The Qur'ān is an intercessor, something given permission to intercede, and it is rightfully believed in. Whoever puts it in front of him, it will lead him to Paradise; whoever puts it behind him, it will steer him to the Hellfire."[4]

About the natural inclination to Islām, Allāh says

"So set you (O Muhammad) your face towards the religion of pure Islāmic Monotheism Hanīfā (worship none but Allāh Alone) Allāh's Fitrah (i.e. Allāh's Islāmic Monotheism), with which He has created mankind. No change let there be in Khalq–illah (i.e. the Religion of Allāh Islāmic Monotheism), that is the straight religion, but most of men know not." - Qur'ān, 30:30

Even more clearly, He informs us about the natural inclination toward knowing good and evil. He said,

"And by Nafs (Ādam or a person or a soul, etc.), and Him Who perfected him in proportion; then He showed him what is wrong for him and what is right for him; indeed he succeeds who purifies his ownself. And indeed he fails who corrupts his ownself" - Qur'ān, 91:7-10

The Prophet Muhammad (PBUH) said:

"Every child is born upon the fitrah (natural disposition), and then his parents make him a Jew, Christian, or Magian, as an animal produces a perfect young animal: do you see any part of its body amputated?"[5]

---

[4] Sunan Ibn Mājah, Hadīth No. 216
[5] Ṣaḥīḥ al-Bukhārī, Hadīth No. 4775

The Best Company

People often ask, *"Where do we find God?" Where does He clearly say He is?* The answer is, without a doubt, on the Straight Path.

"... Verily, my Lord is on the Straight Path (the truth)." - Qur'ān, 11:56

Nearness to Him lies in adhering to the Straight Path and being mindful of Him, even amidst overwhelming distractions. At the end of this path, He has prepared the fulfillment of all our deepest desires in ways beyond our comprehension.

He did not leave us to wander aimlessly or search blindly for this path. Instead, He sent Messengers, one after another, to specific communities, and Prophet Muhammad (PBUH) as a guide for all of humanity. Just as He guided all the Prophets, from the first to the last—Muhammad (peace and blessings of Allāh be upon them all)—the final Prophet, as the Qur'ān says,

"Say (O Muhammad): "Truly, my Lord has guided me to a Straight Path, a right religion, the religion of Ibrahīm (Abraham), Hanīfā [i.e. the true Islāmic Monotheism – to believe in One God (Allāh i.e. to worship none but Allāh, Alone)] and he was not of Al-Mushrikūn " - Qur'ān, 6:161

"Verily, Ibrahīm (Abraham) was an Ummah and he was not one of those who were Al-Mushrikūn (polytheists, idolaters, disbelievers). (He was) thankful for His (Allāh's) Graces. He (Allāh) chose him (as an intimate friend) and guided him to a Straight Path." – Qur'ān, 16:120-121

The Qur'ān conveys the same message about many other prophets, as reflected in these verses.

"It is those who believe (in the Oneness of Allāh and worship none but Him Alone) and confuse not their belief with Zulm (wrong i.e. by worshipping others besides Allāh), for them (only) there is security and they are the guided. And that was Our Proof which We gave Ibrahīm (Abraham) against his people. We raise whom We will in degrees. Certainly your Lord is All-Wise, All-Knowing. And We bestowed upon him Ishāque (Isaac) and Ya'qūb (Jacob), each of them We guided, and before him, We guided Nūh (Noah), and among his progeny Dāwūd (David), Sulaimān (Solomon), Ayyūb (Job), Yūsuf (Joseph), Mūsā (Moses), and Hārūn (Aaron). Thus do We reward the good-doers. And Zakariyā (Zachariya), and Yahyā (John) and 'Īsā (Jesus) and Iliyās (Elias), each one of them was of the righteous. And Ismā'īl (Ishmael) and Al-Yas'a (Elisha), and Yūnus (Jonah) and Lūt (Lot), and each one of them We preferred above the 'Ālamin (mankind and jinns) (of their times). And also some of their fathers and their progeny and their brethren, We chose them, and We guided them to a Straight Path. This is the Guidance of Allāh with which He guides whomsoever He will of His slaves. But if they had joined in worship others with Allāh, all that they used to do would have been of no benefit to them. They are those whom We gave the Book, Al-Hukm (understanding of the religious laws), and Prophethood. But if these disbelieve therein (the Book, Al-Hukm and Prophethood), then, indeed We have entrusted it to a people (such as the Companions of Prophet Muhammad) who are not disbelievers therein. They are those whom Allāh had guided. So follow their guidance. Say: 'No

reward I ask of you for this (the Qur'ān). It is only a reminder for the 'Ālamīn (mankind and jinns).'" - Qur'ān, 6:82-90

We find clear instructions to follow the teachings and examples of the prophets, who were guided by Allāh on the same Straight Path. Through them, He guides humanity, as He says,

"...But We have made it (this Qur'ān) a light wherewith We guide whosoever of Our slaves We will. And verily, you (O Muhammad) are indeed guiding (mankind) to the Straight Path..." – Qur'ān, 42:52-53

The Straight Path is filled with clear, constructive guidance for our worldly affairs. Those who adhere to it understand the proper order of things and are thus spared from confusion. And He also said,

"And certainly, you (O Muhammad) call them to a Straight Path." - Qur'ān, 23:73

This is how Islām explains all other religions: they are divergent paths that lead away from the Straight Path. They consist of misinterpretations, distortions, and the politicization of various divine messages. While some are clearly man-made, many involve people attributing divine status to Allāh's Prophets—titles the Prophets never claimed for themselves.

It is also important to understand that there are different ranks within the Straight Path, and we must all strive to ascend higher, seeking greater closeness to Allāh. The Prophets, despite their own human struggles, were trained through their prophetic journeys. They faced the worst trials and severe opposition. For example, the journey of Prophet Ibrahīm (PBUH) began with curiosity, as Allāh describes,

"When the night covered him over with darkness he saw a star. He said: "This is my lord." But when it set, he said: "I like not those that set.". When he saw the moon rising up, he said: "This is my lord." But when it set, he said: "Unless my Lord guides me, I shall surely be among the erring people.". When he saw the sun rising up, he said: "This is my lord. This is greater." But when it set, he said: "O my people! I am indeed free from all that you join as partners in worship with Allāh." -
Qur'ān, 6:76-78

It all begins with paying attention and asking the right questions. Even after reaching the highest rank on this path, the Prophet Muhammad (PBUH) was known for striving even harder, standing in prayer most of the night until his blessed feet became swollen. When asked why he prayed so intensely despite having his past, present, and future sins forgiven by Allāh, he (PBUH) replied,

"Should I not be a grateful servant?"[6]

He endured the heartache of burying all but one of his children and would often say:

"Whatever Allāh takes is His, and whatever He gives is His, and everything with Him has a limited fixed term (in this world)."[7]

---

[6] Ṣaḥīḥ Muslim, Hadīth No. 2819b
[7] Ṣaḥīḥ Al-Bukhārī, Hadīth No. 6655

He (PBUH) often went without food for days. When he asked his wives if there was any food and they had none, he would choose to fast for the rest of the day rather than complain.

He encouraged hard work and strongly discouraged begging.

Az-Zubayr ibn al-'Awwām (RA) reported that the Prophet (PBUH) said:

"That one of you takes his rope, goes to the mountain, cuts some firewood, carries it on his back, and sells it, thereby Allāh saves his face (his dignity) is better for him than to ask people and they either give him or deny him."[8]

The believer learns from the Prophets, remains connected to their Lord and Creator, and is content with Him, loving Him with all their heart, regardless of their circumstances. Their faith is unshaken, their grip on the Straight Path is firm, and their steadfastness is profound.

Focused, fulfilled, Unafraid, and ever prepared for death, the believer longs for the day they meet their Lord, hoping for His mercy and the attendant reward of everlasting happiness that transcends afterward. In their last breadth, the angel of death welcomes them to their freedom from the pains and worries of this world and into the everlasting peace, tranquility, and promised glory of their creator.

Before engaging in their daily worldly affairs, the believer stands in prayer each morning, offering two volun-

---

[8] Ṣaḥīḥ al-Bukhārī, Hadīth No. 662

tary rak'āts[9] before the Fajr (dawn prayer)—a gift better than the entire world and all it contains.[10]

What greater happiness could the world offer them? What sorrow could possibly take this joy away?

This book alone cannot fully capture the vast teachings of this beautiful religion and way of life—the religion of the Straight Path.

And indeed, Prophet 'Īsā (Jesus, PBUH) said to his people,

"And verily Allāh is my Lord and your Lord. So worship Him (Alone). That is the Straight Path." - Qur'ān, 19:36

---

[9] Each Rak'ah is a unit of prayer in the special daily prayers called as-Salāt

[10] Ṣaḥīḥ Muslim, Ḥadīth No. 725a

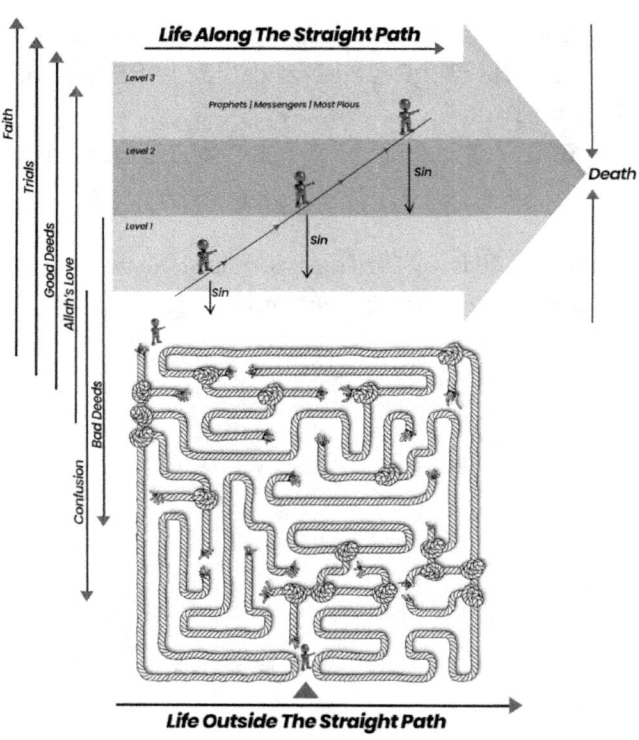

Figure 14.1: *A schematic Diagram Illustrating Life Within and Outside the Straight Path*

About the Author

MUBARAK SULAIMAN UKASHAT hails from the small village of South Ibie in the Iyakpi Kingdom of Edo State, Nigeria. His early education began at Adolor Primary School and Eghosa Grammar School in Benin City. His formal Islāmic education began at the School of Arabic and Islāmic Studies at the Islāmic Center in Afikpo, Ebonyi State, Nigeria, where he studied for six years covering Junior, Middle, and High School. He earned a Bachelor's Degree in Physics from the Federal University of Petroleum Resources and a National Diploma in Petroleum Engineering from the Petroleum Training Institute, both located in Warri, Delta State, Nigeria. In 2016, Mubarak completed a Master's Degree in Physics from King Fahd University of Petroleum and Minerals in Saudi Arabia, where he had the privilege of studying under renowned Islamic scholars in the region for three years. He went on to earn a Ph.D. in Physics from Utah State University, USA, in 2022. He is the Founder of Better Education to Africa (BETA), a nonprofit that helps provide educational materials from the United States to support the education of the poor and needy in Africa. He is also the Founder of Imān Arise; a personal development online media. He has held the position of Imām at a community Islāmic center in Dhahran, Saudi Arabia, as well as at the Logan Islāmic Center in Utah, USA. He is currently focused on writing books in both Islāmic studies and physics, and he also works as a private consultant and businessman.

Mubarak is happily married and the father of four daughters and a son. He loves spending time with family, reading, mentoring, teaching, and playing professional pickleball.

www.ingramcontent.com/pod-product-compliance
Lightning Source LLC
Chambersburg PA
CBHW060910120626
46553CB00001B/277